Efficacy of the Instruments of National Power in Winning Insurgent Warfare: A Case Study Focused on Peru and Sendero Luminoso

Grady S. Taylor

THE EFFICACY OF THE INSTRUMENTS OF NATIONAL POWER IN WINNING
INSURGENT WARFARE: A CASE STUDY FOCUSED ON
PERU AND SENDERO LUMINOSO

A thesis presented to the Faculty of the US Army
Command and General Staff College in partial
fulfillment of the requirements for the
degree

MASTER OF MILITARY ART AND SCIENCE
STRATEGY

by

Grady Scott Taylor, MAJ, USA
B.S., United States Military Academy, West Point, NY 1992

Fort Leavenworth, Kansas
2004

Approved for public release; distribution is unlimited.

MASTER OF MILITARY ART AND SCIENCE

THESIS APPROVAL PAGE

Name of Candidate: Major Grady Scott Taylor

Thesis Title: The Efficacy of the Instruments of National Power in Winning Insurgent Warfare: A Case Study Focused on Peru and Sendero Luminoso

Approved by:

_____, Thesis Committee Chair
Harold S. Orenstein, Ph.D.

_____, Member
Lieutenant Colonel Lisa L. Cranford, M.A.

_____, Member
Major Scott R. Peters, M.A.

Accepted this 18th day of June 2004 by:

_____, Director, Graduate Degree Programs
Robert F. Baumann, Ph.D.

The opinions and conclusions expressed herein are those of the student author and do not necessarily represent the views of the US Army Command and General Staff College or any other governmental agency. (References to this study should include the foregoing statement.)

ABSTRACT

THE EFFICACY OF THE INSTRUMENTS OF NATIONAL POWER IN WINNING INSURGENT WARFARE: A CASE STUDY FOCUSED ON PERU AND SENDERO LUMINOSO, by MAJ Grady Scott Taylor, 149 pages.

Determining the causes of insurgency is important to military studies and social sciences because of the pervasiveness of insurgency and its impact on regional stability and governmental legitimacy. The moderating influences of the Cold War are gone, and insurgent warfare and terrorism are taking on greater importance for the military professional. Insurgent activities range from propaganda and political mobilization to guerrilla warfare and domestic and transnational terrorism. Their goals are even more diverse and complex. By trying to understand how insurgencies become impervious to counterinsurgency efforts, it becomes easier to understand how to prevent their devastating effects on regional stability and international affairs. In order to be successful, any insurgency or counterinsurgency strategy must apply all of the instruments of national power: diplomatic, informational, military and economic. To fail to do so virtually guarantees perpetuation of the struggle and likely greater bloodshed and instability. This thesis provides an in-depth analysis of the Peruvian insurgency Sendero Luminoso and the governmental counterinsurgency efforts between 1980 and 1994 to demonstrate this. Studying what makes insurgencies endure in spite of strong counterinsurgency efforts is vital to preparing the military professional to know his enemy and fight on the modern battlefield.

ACKNOWLEDGMENTS

I would like to thank my distinguished committee for their steadfast advice, mentorship, motivational inspiration, and patience. Without the wisdom of your experience, your patience through my writer's blocks and your guidance in directing my thoughts, this thesis would not have been possible.

I also owe a tremendous debt of endless gratitude to my family (Susan, Courtney, and Matthew) for their patience, assistance, and support. Without their love and support, this project would have been exceedingly insurmountable. To Susan, especially, I owe so much for the hours spent proofreading my writing; your assistance in polishing my language and in simplifying my all-to-often convoluted thoughts was indispensable. Thank you also for "holding down the fort" as I strove to isolate myself from outside distractions and urgent matters in order to focus my thoughts.

TABLE OF CONTENTS

                                                          Page

MASTER OF MILITARY ART AND SCIENCE THESIS APPROVAL PAGE ii

ABSTRACT iii

ACKNOWLEDGMENTS iv

ACRONYMS viii

LIST OF FIGURES ix

LIST OF TABLES x

CHAPTER 1. INTRODUCTION 1

    Prologue 1
    Research Questions 2
    Thesis Organization 2
    Assumptions 3
    Limitations 3
    Delimitations 4
    Significance of the Study 5

CHAPTER 2. LITERATURE REVIEW 7

    Introduction 7
    Material Relevant to General Insurgency Theory 7
    Subject Matter Specific to the Case Study 17

CHAPTER 3. RESEARCH METHODOLOGY 22

    Introduction 22
        Bard O'Neill's Methodology 22
        The Modified Methodology 23
    Setting the Stage 24
        Historical Context 24
        Defining the Environment 24
            The Physical Environment 25
                Terrain 25
                Climate 25
                Transportation-Communication Infrastructure 26
            The Human Environment 26
                Demographic Distribution 26

        Social Structure 27
        Economic Factors 29
        Political Culture and System... 30
    Analyzing the Insurgents 32
        A Brief History of the Insurgent Group 32
        Insurgency Classification... 32
        Insurgency Strategy in Broad Terms 33
        Insurgent Organization 34
            Ideology 34
            Goals 35
            Leadership 36
            Organization... 37
        Insurgent Strategy According to the Instruments of National Power........ 40
            Diplomatic 41
            Informational 42
            Military 44
            Economic 44
    Analyzing the Governmental Response 45
        Governmental Response 45

CHAPTER 4. SETTING THE STAGE FOR THE PERUVIAN CASE STUDY 50

Historical Context 50
Defining the Environment 52
    The Physical Environment 52
        Terrain... 52
        Climate 52
        Transportation-Communications Infrastructure 53
    The Human Environment 54
        Demographic Distribution 54
        Social Structure.. 55
            Historical Proclivity for Violence 55
            Class System and Ethnic Discrimination... 57
            Levels of Education 58
            Levels of Crime 59
        Economic Factors 60
            Disparity between Haves and Have-Nots 60
            Relative Deprivation 61
            Unemployment.. 62
            Poor Health Conditions 63
        Political Culture and System... 63

CHAPTER 5. INSURGENTS AND THE GOVERNMENT.. 70

Analyzing the Insurgents 70
    A Brief History of Sendero 70

    Insurgency Classification 73
    Insurgency Strategy in Broad Terms 74
    Insurgent Organization 76
        Ideology 76
        Goals 77
        Leadership 78
        Organization 81
    Insurgent Strategy According to the Instruments of National Power 85
        1965 to 1980: Before the Violence--Building Consensus and Infrastructure 85
        1980 to 1983: The Formative Years 86
        1983 to 1987: Expanding and Concentrating on Rural Violence 89
        1987 to 1992: Transition to Urban Strategy and Height of Power 92
        1992 to 2002: End of Potency 96
    Analyzing Governmental Response and Strategy 97
        Governmental Response 98
        The Belaúnde Administration (1980 to 1985) 99
        The García Administration (1985 to 1990) 100
        The Fujimori Administration (1990 to 2000) 101

CHAPTER 6. CONCLUSIONS 111

    Conclusions to Be Drawn About the Peruvian Case Study 111
        Diplomatic Instruments of National Power 111
        Informational Instruments of National Power 112
        Military Instruments of National Power 114
        Economic Instruments of National Power 115
    General Conclusions 116
    Suggestions for Future Research 117

GLOSSARY 119

APPENDIX A. FIGURES 125

APPENDIX B. TABLES 129

BIBLIOGRAPHY 132

INITIAL DISTRIBUTION LIST 137

CERTIFICATION FOR MMAS DISTRIBUTION STATEMENT 138

ACRONYMS

APRA	Alianza Popular Revolucionaria Americana - American Popular Revolutionary Alliance
CIA	Central Intelligence Agency
DIME	Diplomatic, Informational, Military, and Economic (instruments of national power)
FM	Field Manual
IU	Izquierda Unida - United Left
JP	Joint Publication
MRTA	Movimiento Revolucionario Túpac Amaru - Revolutionary Movement of Tupac Amaru
PCP	Partido Comunista del Peru - the Communist Party of Peru
RAND	Research And Development (nonprofit research organization)
UHV	Upper Huallaga Valley
UNSCH	University of San Cristobal de Huamanga - the University of San Cristobal in Huamanga

LIST OF FIGURES

Figure 1. Author's Modified Methodology for this Case Study 125

Figure 2. Peruvian Geographical Regions 126

Figure 3. Peruvian Transportation Infrastructure (1991). 127

Figure 4. Peruvian Geographical Map Reflecting Departments 128

LIST OF TABLES

Table 1. Population and Percentage Growth of Major Cities, Census Years 1961-90...129

Table 2. Distribution of Population by Region, Census Years 1940-90........................130

Table 3. Distribution of Income by Quintile, 1972 and 1985..130

Table 4. Health Indicators, 1975-90 131

CHAPTER 1

INTRODUCTION

> I hold it that a little rebellion, now and then, is a good thing, and as necessary in the political world as storms in the physical. . . . It is a medicine necessary for the sound health of government.[1]
>
> Thomas Jefferson, Letter to James Madison

<u>Prologue</u>

Insurrectionist-terrorist rebellion or righteous freedom movement--the distinctions depend entirely on one's belief in the legitimacy of the existing government. Indeed, the study of why men rebel is an important one, particularly in Latin American, because of the significant impact it has had on so many lives, their culture, and society. With the crumbling of the colonial empires and the bipolar conflict between Soviet expansionist communism and American capitalist imperialism, insurgent warfare in regions with little significant strategic value to the world powers spawned and evolved into wars-by-proxy as the superpowers vied for international influence and regional ideological domination.

Insurgency is as old as armed conflict itself, as Roman armies could have reported from Gaul or Judea.[2] Sun Tzu wrote in the late fifth century B.C. about using guerrilla warfare to defeat a superior force. In many cases, the difference between a radical rebel extremist and revered noble patriot is measured only in the success of the movement and who writes the history. At one time, revolutionaries from thirteen mutinous colonies united against a "tyrant" king, using tactics considered as abhorrent in their time as most consider those of Sendero Luminoso. The result of that colonial insurgency is a nation that today stands as the icon for freedom, liberty, and democracy worldwide.

Research Questions

The intent of this study is to research the elemental factors that led to social breakdown in Peru and the strategies employed by both Sendero Luminoso (henceforth referred to as Sendero) and the government in its fight for survival. From this analysis the author will uncover lessons to be drawn about the importance of using all instruments of national power to directly target the goals, strengths, and weaknesses of one's adversary.

The research will focus on understanding insurgent groups that seek regime change, using Peru as a case study, and understanding the relevance of the governmental policies and strategies, geographical characteristics, cultural attributes, economic issues, and informational aspects to these organizations' success or failure. History has shown that some insurgencies are effectively countered and defeated quickly in their early stages, while others are impervious to all efforts of the regime to counter and eliminate them. The primary research question of this thesis is: Using Peru as a case study, can lessons be extracted that can be applied to insurgencies in general to explain why they endure? Secondary questions include: What characteristics of Peru's physical and human environment facilitated the rise of Sendero? What characteristics of the Peruvian insurgency led to its potency? How did the success or failure of Peru's insurgency to use all instruments of national power affect the outcome or duration of the insurgency? How did the success or failure of the Peruvian government's counterinsurgency to use all instruments of national power affect the outcome or duration?

Thesis Organization

The question of why one revolutionary movement succeeds quickly while others abate under the slightest counterinsurgency efforts has been a popular topic of research.

Explanations of why insurgencies endure in the face of staunch resistance however are less prevalent. The first chapter introduces the dilemma of enduring insurgencies in Latin America, conveys the research questions, establishes the assumptions necessary for this thesis, defines critical terms, explains the limitations of the research and the delimitations imposed by the author, and explicates the significance of this research. Chapter 2 outlines the relevant academic work covering insurgency. Chapter 3 outlines the methodology adopted by the author for this study, focusing on those factors essential to the analysis of insurgency. Chapter 4 covers the Peruvian setting while chapter 5 outlines the realities of Sendero and analyzes the use of the instruments of national power by both the insurgents and the government in accordance with the methodology in chapter 3. The final chapter provides the conclusions drawn from the research on the factors that foment long-standing militant insurgencies and provides topics for future research.

Assumptions

Some elemental assumptions are necessary to complete this study. The first is that through the study of multiple resources, the true motives of some of these complex organizations can be realistically determined. An additional assumption is that insurgent forces commit political violence with hopes of attaining or achieving specific goals and do not fight just for the sake of bloodlust or vengeance.

Limitations

Some limitations will affect the scope of this study. Insurgencies are decidedly complex and because the reasons for failures are emotionally charged, accurate explanations for failures of insurgents and counterinsurgents, particularly from those directly involved, are elusive. The lack of primary source material from the insurgent groups and their leaders will also limit the research. As Henry Dietz asserts in his essay, "Revolutionary Organization in the Countryside: Peru," because of its ideology and reclusive leadership, "Sendero Luminoso is among the world's most closed movements: it publishes virtually nothing of its own, it grants no interviews, it seldom claims credit for its activities, and its members and adherents are sworn to secrecy."[3] In spite of this, there are a few first-hand interviews with the some of the more junior insurgents that can be used to ensure this analysis captures both sides of the dispute but by and large very little material is available from Sendero leadership.

Delimitations

This thesis is delimited by the use of only one specific case study--the lessons to be extracted from the Peruvian experience. In using only one case study, the author was able to conduct a more detailed analysis and follow a more comprehensive methodology to facilitate a better isolation of the factors that promulgated one of the longest-standing and most ruthless insurgencies in Latin America and the world. The very nature of the endurance and brutality of Sendero in the face of a long counterinsurgency campaign and the fact that the government did finally succeed makes it an excellent choice for investigating the causes for such a lasting revolution. Admittedly, by limiting the study to one case study, there is a reduced universal applicability of the findings because some characteristics of this insurgency are idiosyncratic to Peru and its struggle. Indeed, some argue that Sendero is unique among insurgents throughout history, but in terms of use of the DIME, there is still efficacy in the analysis.

Though extremely relevant in light of the changing nature of insurgency today, urban insurgency theory and urban warfare were less relevant in the Peruvian case study and Sendero Luminoso until its latter years and even then only marginally as a lesser component of its overall rural campaign. As such, though the urban component of many modern insurgencies has captured the attention of many interested in modern insurgency warfare, it is not addressed in much detail with respect to this case study.

Significance of the Study

Insurgency remains one of the most ubiquitous forms of warfare and presents a crucial challenge to the international community, governments, and the military. As Ted Gurr noted in his book, *Why Men Rebel?*, "political violence is a pervasive phenomenon . . . few contemporary or historical societies have been free of it for long."[4] The study and understanding of insurgency is imperative to military professionals, especially those seeking to remain relevant in the contemporary operational environment. Insurgency is an integral part of the spectrum of conflict. Many have argued that future conflicts facing the US Army will cover a diverse range of possibilities across the spectrum of conflict. Most argue that the US will likely be endangered by threats from the center of the spectrum of conflict: terrorist attacks, insurgent activity, and regional conflict. The US and its allies hold a monopoly on the most powerful military means in the world, with no adversary capable of conventionally countering their sheer combined military and economic strength. Nevertheless, the US still has many enemies who are fundamentally, ideologically, and vehemently opposed to its beliefs. Recent history has shown that the US is increasingly finding that its adversaries choose unconventional methods to attack it. These attacks may be aimed at the US directly or indirectly through its allies. The whole point of insurgency is to defeat a superior force by fighting on terms of the insurgent's own choosing--to attack the enemy asymmetrically, matching strength against vulnerability. The ability to counter an enemy who fights asymmetrically is now far more relevant and important.

This is not new to the US military. Indeed, it has been relevant for quite some time. President John F. Kennedy once said,

> There is another type of warfare--new in its intensity, ancient in its origin--war by guerrillas, subversives, insurgents, assassins; war by ambush instead of by combat, by infiltration instead of aggression, seeking victory by eroding and exhausting the enemy instead of engaging him. . . . It prays on unrest. . . . Our forces, therefore, must fulfill a broader role, as a complement to our diplomacy, as an army of our diplomacy, as a deterrent to our adversaries, and as a symbol to our allies of our determination to support them.[5]

The struggle to understand insurgency is not new but it is far more important to military professionals today than previously due to the increasing tendency of American politicians to send the military to fight on asymmetric battlefields to exercise its role as the sole superpower and to propagate American democratic values worldwide. Both joint and Army doctrine recognize this new trend and have included both the support for and countering of insurgency as an integral part of the military professional's mission.

---

[1] James Morton Smith, ed., *Thomas Jefferson to James Madison The Republic of Letters: The Correspondence between Thomas Jefferson and James Madison 1776-1826*, vol. 1 (New York, NY: W. W. Norton and Company, 1995), 461.

[2] Bard E. O'Neill, *Insurgency and Terrorism: Inside Modern Revolutionary Warfare* (McLean, VA: Brassey's Publishing, 1990), 1.

[3] Barry M. Schutz, and Robert O. Slater, *Revolution and Political Change in the Third World* (Boulder, CO: Lynne Rienner Publishers, 1990), 119.

[4] Ted Robert Gurr, *Why Men Rebel* (Princeton, NJ: Princeton University Press, 1970), 8.

[5] US Army. Headquarters, Department of the Army, Field Manual 3-07, *Stability Operations and Support Operations* (Washington, DC: US Government Printing Office, February 2003), 3-3.

CHAPTER 2

LITERATURE REVIEW

<u>Introduction</u>

This chapter provides an overview of modern insurgency theory and summarizes the influential works researched for this thesis in order to gain an appreciation for the breadth and depth of existing material. What is clear is that there is an expansive amount of open source governmental, academic, and periodical literature available that analyzes revolution, and insurgency on a broad spectrum, ranging from general conceptual and theoretical perspectives to specific analyses of discrete insurgencies. Some resources are somewhat dated and many proffer conflicting arguments on the true origins, causes, ideologies, typologies, and theories of insurgency. However, the sources below highlight those materials that were deemed most relevant and important to the analysis of modern Latin American insurgency, and particularly to understanding the causes of enduring insurgencies. This literature review is separated into two parts: the first focuses on those texts that provide a more general explanation for the understanding and classification of insurgency, while the second part focuses on those sources selected to better understand the insurgency in Peru.

<u>Material Relevant to General Insurgency Theory</u>

Contrary to common popular Western misperceptions, insurgency is not a uniquely communist phenomenon; however, some communists have developed the most significant theoretical works on the subject. Insurgency theory can be separated into four broad categories: Marxist-Leninist conspiratorial strategy; Mao Tse-tung's strategy of protracted popular war; military-focus strategy, typified by Fidel Castro, Regis Debray and Che Guevara; and the urban warfare strategy advocated by Carlos Marighella.[1] Historians and social scientists have argued the relevance and applicability in Latin America of each of these four strategies. Sendero has exhibited characteristics of all four strategies throughout its existence. The following texts serve as the bedrock of this thesis's research to facilitate understanding of Latin American insurgency.

Insurgency and Terrorism: Inside Modern Revolutionary Warfare by Bard O'Neill (1990). In this landmark text, Bard O'Neill offers a framework through which to analyze insurgencies, past, present, and future. He argues articulately why insurgencies are likely to remain a key level of conflict in the future. The author systemically dissects insurgency and terrorism so that one may understand its causes, effects, and the nature of revolutionary warfare. He examines the strategist's ways, means, and ends and lays out a clear framework to understand the source of a particular conflict. O'Neill goes on to examine various strategies used by revolutionaries and insurgents and delves into the theoretical, discussing theories of revolution, including Lenin's conspiratorial strategy, Mao's protracted popular war strategy, Guevara's military-focus strategy, and Carlos Marighella's urban-centric strategy.[2] Providing a superb means for classifying the sources of insurgency, he discusses factors including: the physical and human environment, relevance of popular and external support, the importance of effective governmental response, insurgent organization, and the political conditions that create the atmosphere for insurgency. He uses historical examples to illustrate specific points throughout his work, discussing the Spanish guerrillas who combated Napoleon's invasion, the American guerilla revolutionary effort of the Swamp Fox (Francis Marion), and Soviet partisans attacking the Nazi invaders. As O'Neill points out, no framework for analysis can be perfect, but his text provides a superb beginning.[3] As chapter 3 will show, the analysis of this thesis hinges on a methodology based on O'Neill's framework.

State Failure Task Force Report (2000). Begun in 1994, this report identified the primary factors that lead to social breakdown and provided models that, when applied to historical data, classified stable countries and countries headed for state failure with reportedly 70-to-80-percent accuracy.[4] Several conditions were associated with varying types of state failure and with failure in many different global regions, including: quality of life, regime type, international influences, and ethnic or religious composition of a country or its leadership.[5] Other aspects, such as patterns of development, types of ideology, and the number of years a political leader spent in office, were also presented as important.[6] The focus is on actual state failure in accordance with four types presented in the report: revolutionary wars, ethnic wars, adverse regime changes, and genocides and politicides.[7] Although this analysis seems to capture most of the key issues relevant to state failure, it fails to address several key additional determinants that are captured in Bard O'Neill's analysis with respect to the geographical and human environment that make hostile insurgent rebellion more likely. Additionally, a natural bias toward pluralistic societies in this report is apparent. As in the case of Peru, democracy is not necessarily the panacea of insurgency. Democracy may be a strong deterrent to state failure but it is clearly not a deterrent to vicious insurgencies; in fact, the openness and freedom of democracies often makes it easier for insurgencies to flourish. The report provides a good framework for the analysis of some insurgencies, but requires elaboration for the understanding of an enduring insurgency like Sendero.

Distant Thunder: Patterns of Conflict in the Developing World by Donald Snow (1997). Written after the collapse of the old bipolar world order, this text accurately points out the increased relevance of the study of insurgency as an even more important threat to global stability. Separatist movements, horrific genocidal ethnic conflicts, chaotic violence in failing states, and criminal insurgencies are an integral part of the new world order with which the developed world is going to have to deal. Donald Snow outlines the kind of societies in which insurgency is most likely to occur. He appropriately asserts that incentive to engage in insurgent warfare exists when societal misery prevails, and that contributing factors that make one state more prone to insurgency include political illegitimacy, economic deprivation, intercommunal hatred, and geographical isolation.[8] His insight into why the number of developing countries in which these conditions exist far exceeds the number of countries that have successful ongoing insurgencies is shrewd. Snow focuses on more than just the conditions that make revolts likely; he also looks at the need for some growth and prosperity to make revolution even possible. He aptly cites Crane Brinton's *The Anatomy of Revolution*, "Insurrectionary violence is more likely to occur in societies experiencing some growth and wealth, but where the majority finds itself outside that success."[9]

On Guerilla Warfare by Mao Tse-tung (1992). Since its first introduction in 1961, this text has been one of the mainstays of revolutionary and military literature. Mao Tse-tung's treatise is the bible to revolutionary adherents of protracted popular war. Included in the version used for this thesis are two introductions to Mao's thoughts, explained in the first edition by British Brigadier General Samuel Griffith and in the second edition by the two professors of history Arthur Waldron and Colonel Edward O'Dowd.

To some, the book may appear to be a mere manual of irregular tactics, but in reality this text provides much more. At the core of understanding Mao's writing is his realization that social and political considerations are inseparable from revolution, and that they must take priority over military considerations.[10] According to Mao, social revolution and mobilization of the people are indispensable to successful insurgency and revolutionary leaders must be prepared to spend considerable time and effort to foster this popular support. In this text, Mao outlines a three-phased strategy for protracted popular war, focusing on the strategic imperatives of judicious and progressive development of decisive military, political, and social power to the point where revolutionary leaders are eventually capable of attacking the existing government as equals or from a position of strength.[11] The first phase of the three-phased strategy is strategic retreat, in which the weaker insurgents conserve their strength and build the basis for their offensive strategy; the revolutionary leaders consolidate forces and mobilize popular support. The second stage is one of equilibrium or strategic stalemate, wherein insurgent forces develop sufficient capabilities to attack the government directly but do not have sufficient strength to take the regime on as equals. The final stage is one where the insurgent movement organizes itself into conventional forces with regular armies capable of deliberate and direct large-scale attacks on the governmental military as a peer competitor.[12]

Guerrilla Warfare by Che Guevara (1985). Che Guevara's amazing life story has lifted him to legendary status. The hero of the 1959 revolution in Cuba, Guevara believed that revolution would also topple many other imperialist governments in Latin America. His call to action, his persona of invincibility, and his influential writings on military-focused strategy continue to affect the course of Latin American history and international relations. This edition of Guevara's classic work, originally penned in 1961, contains the text of his book, as well as two later essays titled "Guerrilla Warfare: A Method" and "Message to the Tri-continental." Also included is a detailed introduction by Brian Loveman and Thomas M. Davies Jr. examining Guevara's text, his political impact, the situation in Latin America, and the US response to events in Latin America. Loveman and Davies provide in-depth case studies that apply Guevara's theories on revolution to political situations in seven Latin American countries, helping one to better understand Guevara's theoretical contribution to revolutionary literature.

Che Guevara placed significant import on the use of military victories, focusing on guerrilla hit-and-run tactics, to erode the government's resolve and ability to suppress the insurgency.[13] The author gives primacy to the value of asymmetrical armed attacks and subordinates political considerations to the military strategy. Guevara's strategy is predicated on a firm commitment to socialist revolution through armed struggle directed by a revolutionary vanguard.[14] Guevara does not categorically discount the value of popular support, but, unlike Mao Tse-tung, he does not see it as a necessary antecedent to military insurrection.[15] According to the author, sustained efforts to acquire popular support are useful when possible, but it is more likely that through judicious application of military force the government can first be de-legitimized and the insurgents can thereby erode popular support for the government. Guevara uses the example of the Cuban Revolution to demonstrate three principles central to his strategy: (1) popular forces can win a war against the Army, (2) it is not necessary to wait until all conditions for making revolution are present because the revolutionary vanguard can create those conditions, and (3) in the underdeveloped regions of Latin America, the countryside is the basic area for armed fighting.[16]

Insurgent Era by Richard Sanger (1967). In this book, Richard Sanger wrote one of the first significant studies on the tactics, goals, and causes of over three hundred insurgencies. In his text, he traces the indicators of rebellion and the primary causes of revolution: nationalism, anticolonialism, and a desire for independence; political injustice or tyranny; economic maladjustment; military imbalance; and the stress of modernization.[17] Though relevant at the time, his work omits several key considerations. His definition of economic maladjustment fails to capture what occurs when a country has a significant disparity between the economic elite and the general population, but has an altruistic ruling regime that seeks to enhance the economic growth of the nation through an influx of capital and resources and is receptive to economic change. In these cases, despite the economic discrepancy, the progressive improvements, even slow ones, foster perceptions of opportunity for improvement that help quell rebellion.

Likewise, in the modern era, anticolonialism and a desire for independence play a much smaller role in the scheme of insurgencies, since the majority of the colonial empires dissolved in Latin America in the early nineteenth century. Whereas colonialism in Latin America by foreign powers is nonexistent today, many Latin American insurgent groups vehemently oppose efforts by their governments toward economic development and globalization on the grounds that such measures invite foreign powers to exploit the resources and people of their countries in a form of economic imperialism. His description of the influence of economic maladjustment and stress of efforts to modernize are particularly relevant to understanding Latin American insurgency.

Insurgency, by Andrew Mackay Scott (1970). Andrew Scott outlines four preconditions for insurgency: hostility to the controlling political or military power; the existence of a discontented elite willing to provide organization and leadership; a widespread acknowledgement of the necessity to use force; and acceptance of violence to achieve political goals, and the capacity to conduct insurgent conflict.[18] Although he captures some key relevant conditions, he overlooks the significance of geographical, societal, and demographical factors. Scott's first and fourth points are valid, although not very descriptive or comprehensive, and his second and third points are not always valid. The insurgency in Peru demonstrates a people's war that required no assistance from a discontented elite. The experience of Castro in the Cuban revolution refutes Scott's third point and is best countered in Che Guevara's book, _Guerilla Warfare_: "Insurgent leaders do not have to wait for the preconditions of insurgency to appear, because they can act to catalyze existing grievances required for positive action . . . thirty or fifty men are adequate to start an armed rebellion."[19]

Why Men Rebel by Ted Gurr (1970). In this book, evidence and theories from the human sciences are brought together to clarify the sources of political violence, when it is likely to occur, and in what form. Gurr's work is less concerned with the classification, and phases of revolutionary warfare than it is with the fundamental reasons that impel men to violence. His work places a greater emphasis on the psychological dimension of revolution, focusing on the causal relationship between perceptions of relative deprivation and rebellion that ensues, exhaustively defining relative deprivation.[20] His book dwells at length on socioeconomic considerations and the reality of rising expectations when faced with governmental inability to meet those expectations.

Ironically, Latin American history is replete with examples where governments pursue extensive economic development to counter insurgent calls for revolution based on relative deprivation. Unfortunately, in some cases, such efforts expose the populace to higher expectations only to discover that the road to becoming a developed nation is a long one and that austerity measures required by international financiers force governments to make conditions worse before they improve. In the face of rising expectations, this is often a daunting task, eroding popular support for the government. The role of ideology, the importance of organization, and the uses and abuses of force as more general circumstances of rebellion are also analyzed.

Gurr's model for rebellion is extremely complex. To simplify it somewhat, it can be summed up in three primary variables: potential for political violence, potential for collective violence, and magnitude of political violence.[21] The first two variables act upon the last. He argues that seven secondary variables impact on the primary variables: intensity of relative deprivation, scope of relative deprivation, intensity of normative justification for violence, intensity of utilitarian justification for violence, scope of justifications for political violence, balance of insurgent and regime coercion, and balance of insurgent and regime institutional support.[22] Essentially, the central contribution of Gurr's argument is that there is a distinctive causal sequence that occurs whereby the development of discontent followed by the introduction of intellectual and charismatic revolutionary leadership, leads to the politicization of that discontent, which ultimately leads to political violence against the regime.[23] If discontented people have constructive means to attain their social and material goals, few will resort to violence.

Political violence is often employed by unreasonable men but is seldom employed without reason.[24] Ted Gurr's book helps explain why individuals to resort to violence.

Reluctant Rebels: Comparative Studies of Revolution by John Walton (1984). Accepting theoretical arguments from other works that emphasize the importance of international capitalism to revolution, Walton insists on the need to introduce political variables into the causal analysis of why insurgencies form. Like Gurr, he stresses the importance of combined economic and political factors that are crucial in precipitating revolutions. Using several revolutions from around the world that occurred during the 1950s, Walton emphasizes the preeminence of economic failure in fomenting revolutions. In each of his case studies he illustrates how disruption from economic reorganization, when tied with failed policy resulting from corrupt, inept, or at least unskilled leadership, can incite insurgencies. A believer in the theory of class struggles, as opposed to simply peasant insurrection, Walton emphasizes the conflict between the elite ruling regime and the lower class have-nots as the true source of rebellion. National revolutions, Walton argues, result from societal conditions that interact with the international political economy. The reality of the ever-expanding global economy, which brings greater hope and prosperity to many but not all, has led some disenchanted segments of many societies, particularly in Latin America, to seek alternative means to achieve the economic and societal status which they have previously been denied. In most cases, this struggle results in insurgency movements. Unlike some of the other analyses of insurgency theorists, Walton is unwilling to separate insurgency movements from outside factors. He skillfully weaves into the fabric of analysis of internal revolutions the understanding of the impact of external influences and the global environment into the struggle for economic and societal self-actualization.

Subject Matter Specific to the Case Study

The Shining Path and Peruvian Terrorism by Gordon H. McCormick (1987). Gordon McCormick, a Latin American expert working for RAND, specializes in Peru and Sendero. In this, his first large-scale work on the impact of Sendero, he provides an in-depth analysis of revolution in Peru and insights into how Senedero was winning the war in Peru in spite of limited popular support for the movement. At that time, Sendero was an effective terrorist organization in Peru, rooted in a combination of Andean mysticism, Maoism, and the unique worldview of its leader. Sendero called for the abolition of a national market economy, industry, the banking system, all foreign trade, and the use of currency, and for the establishment of a communal, village-oriented economy based on a barter exchange system. McCormick did predict in 1987 that Sendero would be unlikely to ever succeed in overthrowing Peru's fragile democracy.

The Shining Path and the Future of Peru by Gordon H. McCormick (1990). This report updates and expands on McCormick's previous work. In this report he examines the continued threat to Peruvian stability posed by Sendero and the degree to which this problem was exacerbated by economic and political crisis. Reiterating some of his earlier work, the author discusses the Shining Path, its genesis, organization, the sources of its support, the movement's governing doctrine and theory of victory, and the makeup of its rural and urban campaigns. He then evaluates those factors that were likely to determine the direction, growth, and prospects of the insurgency in the future; the potential and limits of the Peruvian Army; the nature of the country's economic and associated political crises in the early 1990s; and the net strengths and weaknesses of the Sendero. Finally, he makes judgments about what these trends could mean for the future of Peru.

Revolution and Political Change in the Third World by Barry Schutz and Robert Slater (1990). Barry Schutz and Robert Slater provide an in-depth look at revolutionary movements in the Third World, beginning with a framework for analysis. At the outset, the authors argue that revolutionary movements in developing countries are all motivated by a common perception of regime illegitimacy spawned by deprivation of economic equality, lack of opportunity, and civil rights violations. Extensive discussions of Huntington's distinction between "Western" and "Eastern" types of revolution set the stage for a detailed discussion of the importance of pre-legitimacy once movements begin to gain power.[25] Next it focuses on historical, theoretical, and international factors in revolutionary change in the Third World, outlining the works of four key authors in previous works including: Gerard Chailand's historical approach; T. David Mason's internal-structural approach; William Foltz's external-structural view; and Zaki Laidi's theory weighting the importance of external ideology in influencing Third World regime legitimacy.[26] The remainder focuses on seven types of revolutionary movements that spawn from regime legitimacy disputes. The authors provide a case study that embodies each of the types. Most useful to this thesis was chapter six, which portrays Peru's struggle against Sendero as a model of the third type of legitimacy-based insurgency.

Revolutionary Movements in Latin America by Cynthia McClintock (2001). Cynthia McClintock makes a compelling argument that it takes more than just democratic liberalism to successfully win the fight against some insurgencies. McClintock concedes that the historical record and prevailing popular theory suggest "democracy stymies social revolution."[27] She points out that "not one elected regime has been overthrown by a Marxist guerilla movement – at any time, in any place in the world."[28] In the remainder of her book, however, she explains how three insurgent movements in Latin America – the Farabundo Marti' National Liberation Front in El Salvador, the various insurgencies in Colombia, and Sendero in Peru – have been able to perpetuate their protracted revolutions in spite of the liberal democracy in their respective countries. The interesting question that McClintock's analysis suggests is why these insurgencies have endured in spite of the cure-all of genuine democracy, popularly ascribed by most social scientists.

Vanguard Revolutionaries in Latin America by James F Rochlin (2003). In this text, Rochlin provides an extremely current and thorough review of the status of four insurgencies in Latin America, providing a comprehensive review of the motivations and capabilities of the Mexican Zapatistas, Sendero, the Fuerzas Armadas Revolucionarias de Colombia and the Ejército de Liberacion Nacional. The author explains that, although numerous texts focus on the reasons why men rebel, their focus is on how men rebel.[29] As such, the value of this text to this research lies more in the facts and analysis of the insurgencies analyzed in this study. Rochlin's book devotes two chapters each to these case studies. The first chapter analyzes the guerrilla's origins, ideology, and support base, while the second chapter examines the rebels in relation to power strategy and security.[30]

---

[1]Bard E. O'Neill, *Insurgency and Terrorism: Inside Modern Revolutionary Warfare* (McLean, VA: Brassey's Publishing, 1990), 32-46.

[2]Ibid., 32-46.

[3]Ibid., 11

[4]Central Intelligence Agency, *State Failure Task Force Report* (Washington, D.C.: Central Intelligence Agency, 2000), v.

[5]Ibid., v.

[6]Ibid., vi.

[7]Ibid., iv.

[8]Donald Snow, *Distant Thunder: Patterns in Conflict in the Developing World* (Armonk, NY: M. E. Sharpe, 1997), 59.

[9]Crane Brinton, *The Anatomy of Revolution* (New York, NY: Vantage Publishers, 1965), 33.

[10]Mao Tse-Tung, *On Guerilla Warfare*, introduction and translation by Samuel B. Griffin II (Baltimore, MD: The Nautical and Aviation Publishing Company, 1992), 16.

[11]Ibid., 18.

[12]Ibid., 18-20.

[13]Brian Loveman and Thomas M. Davies, *Guerilla Warfare: Case Histories of Guerilla Movements and Political Change* (Lincoln, NB: University of Nebraska Press, 1985), 10.

[14]Ibid., 11.

[15]Ibid., 11.

[16]Ernesto "Che" Guevara, Guerilla Warfare, in *Guerilla Warfare: Case Histories of Guerilla Movements and Political Change*, eds. Brian Loveman and Thomas M. Davies (Lincoln, NB: University of Nebraska Press, 1985), 47.

[17] Richard H. Sanger, *Insurgent Era* (Washington, D.C.: Potomac Books, Inc. Publishers, 1967), 10.

[18]Andrew M. Scott, *Insurgency* (Chapel Hill, NC: University of North Carolina Press, 1970), 42.

[19]Guevara, *Guerilla Warfare*, 47.

[20]Ted Robert Gurr, *Why Men Rebel* (Princeton, NJ: Princeton University Press, 1970), 12.

[21]Ibid., 8.

[22]Ibid., 320.

[23]Ibid., 12-13.

[24] Ibid., x.

[25] Barry M. Schutz and Robert O. Slater, *Revolution and Political Change in the Third World* (Boulder, CO: Lynne Rienner Publishers, 1990), 8-10.

[26] Ibid., 10-11.

[27] Cynthia McClintock, *Revolutionary Movements in Latin America: El Salvador's FMLN and Peru's Shining Path* (Washington, D.C.: United States Institute Peace Press, 1998), 4.

[28] Ibid., 6.

[29] James F. Rochlin, *Vanguard Revolutionaries in Latin America* (Boulder, CO: Lynne Rienner Publishers, 2003), 2.

[30] Ibid., 19.

CHAPTER 3

RESEARCH METHODOLOGY

Introduction

A number of excellent models exist for understanding and analyzing insurgencies. Some have been discussed in the previous chapter. One of the simpler and most practical methodologies for analyzing modern insurgencies is provided by Bard O'Neill, the Director of Studies of Internal Warfare and Terrorism at the National War College. In his book, *Insurgency and Terrorism: Inside Modern Revolutionary Warfare*, O'Neill highlights two kinds of writings available in the study of insurgency: descriptive and theoretical. Most works are focused on singular aspects and lack the necessary comprehensive coverage of the factors and strategies of insurgencies and the governments that combat them.[1] One of the best attributes of his work is that he focuses on developing a simple methodology for analyzing virtually any insurgency and successfully provides a less theoretical and more practical method of analysis. Because he sought to keep his work succinct, however, there are a few omissions. In addition, the organization of his methodology does not flow as smoothly as it should. His paradigm is nonetheless a superb starting point and is used as the basis for this thesis's methodology, with slight modifications. This chapter will explain this modified methodology.

Bard O'Neill's Methodology

O'Neill's methodology follows a distinct seven-step process. The first step describes the nature of insurgency, classifying the type of insurgency involved, identifying its goals, and determining the political resources and military means used by insurgencies in attaining those goals. He continues by describing the form of warfare adopted by the insurgency, whether terrorism, guerilla warfare, or conventional warfare.[2] His second step focuses on determining the strategic approach of the insurgent group, including conspiratorial, protracted popular war, military-focus, or urban warfare strategy.[3] In his third step, he looks at evaluating the environment in terms of its physical (including terrain, climate, and transportation-communication systems) and human (including demography, socioeconomic conditions, and the political culture of the system) components.[4] O'Neill's fourth step transitions from the environmental factors to an analysis of the popular support that insurgencies strive for in order to guarantee their success and prop up their legitimacy at the expense of the legitimacy of the government.[5] Fifth, the organization and unity of the insurgency are analyzed to determine the ability of the insurgents "to compensate for the material superiority of their opponents."[6] Sixth, he analyzes the external support provided to the insurgent group as a key and critical determinant to insurgencies' chances of success. O'Neill asserts, "Unless governments are utterly incompetent . . . insurgent groups normally must obtain outside assistance if they are to succeed."[7] Finally, step seven analyzes the governmental response in terms of what it can do, what it attempts to do, and how it performs because of the relevance that governmental strategies have on the insurgent group's chances for success and survival.[8]

The Modified Methodology

Though his steps are sound and relevant in most cases, O'Neill's organization omits some important factors. For instance, he does not fully address the importance of historical context in setting the tradition or culture that may foster insurgencies in a country. A country that has a longstanding culture of resorting to violence as a legitimate means for resolving differences is more likely to be predisposed to insurgencies.

Additionally, he does not completely recognize the access that the insurgents have to the instruments of power that the government has. His analysis focuses on insurgent use of political and military tools and misses diplomatic, informational, and economic strategies. The methodology of this thesis heavily utilizes the concepts found in O'Neill's work while reorganizing them into a framework of three phases of analysis: setting the stage for the Peruvian case study, analyzing the insurgents and their strategies, and analyzing the governmental response. By reorganizing O'Neill's steps into three phases and adding the analysis of insurgent and governmental use of the instruments of national power, this author seeks to develop a better structure for analyzing enduring insurgencies with a better structure to answer the primary thesis question (see figure 1 in appendix A).

Setting the Stage

Historical Context

As the famous aphorism by George Santayana goes, "Those who cannot remember the past are condemned to repeat it."[9] To better understand the causes for a certain phenomenon, the history of a country, its people, and its culture must first be grasped to provide the context from which to gain a complete appreciation for its causes. Therefore, the first step is to review a brief history of the development of the country, the cultural experience of its people, and the formation of its government. Though O'Neill alludes to the importance of history, he does not explicitly outline its use as an essential step in analyzing insurgencies; it will be added as the first step in this methodology.

Defining the Environment

The physical and human environments of a country significantly influence the likelihood that potent militant insurgencies will form. In spite of this, none of these individual factors are universally more important than any other in the case of all insurgencies but their analysis can help predict the likelihood of the formation of an insurgency and its chances for success.

The Physical Environment

Terrain

The geography of a country plays an important role in determining how accessible the country is to the government. Complex terrain facilitates insurgencies because it mitigates the relative technological advantages of the government. In open, exposed terrain, insurgents have much greater difficulty concealing themselves from counterinsurgency efforts. Essential to the formation of potent insurgencies are safe havens, either within the country or in adjacent countries. In a country characterized by rugged terrain, including vast jungles, swamps, forests, and mountains, insurgents are better able to avoid governmental forces and control the timing and location of their encounters with counterinsurgency forces to those times when they have the advantage. In some cases, extensive complex urban terrain can also provide similar obstacles to governmental interdiction. The advantages of favorable terrain for guerrilla warfare however are sometimes limited by size and proximity. Small safe havens can be isolated and turned into military free-fire zones, allowing systematic elimination of the insurgents.[10] When complex terrain is plentiful but widespread, it is more difficult to build large, unified groups and to command, control, and synchronize their activities.

Climate

Climate can affect insurgents and government forces alike. Harsher weather tends to favor insurgents, who rely less on technology and transportation, allowing them to more easily escape detection and evade capture. Forces who rely on transportation to respond rapidly to intelligence on insurgent activities may be hindered by harsh weather, making it easier for insurgents to attack in these conditions.

Transportation-Communication Infrastructure

Countries with a robust transportation-communication infrastructure tend to favor the government. When governmental forces are able to move freely and quickly throughout the country, they can react more rapidly. When complex communications networks, such as cell phone or radio repeaters, are available to the government, they are better able to coordinate their forces. As Gurr points out, "guerrilla war is common in underdeveloped countries because of poor transportation and communication networks and the isolation of rural areas, which facilitate guerilla incursions . . . free access to rural people enables guerrillas to propagandize, control, and secure support from them."[11] When the primary means and conduits for information dissemination are controlled by the state and are far reaching, governments are generally better able to prop up their legitimacy, counter the insurgents' information campaigns, and demonize the insurgents.

The Human Environment

Demographic Distribution

The human environment is even more important than the physical environment. Demographics have a major influence on the formation and endurance of insurgencies. When the population of a country is concentrated in cities, the government is likely to have greater control and influence over them and will be more successful at deterring popular support for insurgents. In countries with widely dispersed populations and large segments isolated from urban majorities, insurgencies can fester in remote areas that are cut off from mainstream society. Insurgent leaders are able to use these isolated areas to spread their information campaign, fostering disenchantment with the government. Urban insurgencies can and do exist, and some are successful, but when populations are not overly sympathetic to the insurgent cause, insurgents will find themselves challenged to thrive in the metropolises which are predominantly controlled by the government.

Social Structure

The social structure is especially important. Some countries have a proclivity to resort to violence based on a long-standing history of revering militancy. In these cases, the chances of resorting to violence to resolve differences and overcome disenchantment with the regime are significantly greater. In some societies, violence is such an integral part of life that the populace is desensitized to the tragedies. They grow more concerned with governmental inability to protect than with blaming the insurgents who perpetrate the attacks. In such conditions, insurgents can rapidly gain the lead in their campaign to undermine the government's legitimacy.

Those societies that have distinct divisions between classes or castes lend themselves to greater perceptions of interminable inequity. In these cases, insurgents strive to cast the government as perpetuators of that inequity and spread propaganda that the government is more interested in its own welfare and power than the needs and interests of the people. Societies where upward mobility is possible across social levels and where one can realize a dream based on individual effort or merit are less likely to foster insurgencies--this is the basic premise of democracy and part of the reason for Western society's dogmatic adherence to liberal democratic ideals. "Societal cleavages along racial, ethnic, and religious lines are frequently among the root causes of insurgency and can be either helpful or detrimental to the progression of an insurrection."[12] When one racial, ethnic, or religious segment of society benefits from a disproportionate amount of power over another, then insurgents are more likely to capitalize on that inequity and erode government legitimacy. In some circumstances, however, the existence of smaller minorities may not be advantageous to insurgencies. Efforts by the government may "galvanize support against [the minorities] by emphasizing ancient antagonisms and the threats that the minorities pose to the privileges of the majority."[13] Additionally, where multiple distinct and hostile minorities exist, divisions and animosities among these minorities may actually hinder a cooperative effort against the government and undermine insurgencies. Insurgencies often split on the basis of perceived irreconcilable differences, most often centered on personalities and beliefs, but at times also based on irreconcilable differences stemming from cleavages based on race, ethnicity, or religion. Conversely, when governments or the majorities that they represent overtly discriminate against certain parts or whole segments of society, insurgents are much more likely to find popular support.

One facet of the human environment that O'Neill fails to adequately capture is the relevance of literacy and education. Typically, in every insurgency, there are a number of key intellectuals who are capable of charismatically articulating the ideology of the insurgency and persuasively convincing their followers and portions of the populace to support their insurgent movement. In these cases, when literacy is high and the majority of the masses are better educated, such efforts are often thwarted by the population's preference for seeking alternative means for resolving differences. Higher education levels typically coincide with better access to certain media in the country and often allows for a more informed populace who are less susceptible to propaganda campaigns by insurgents. Additionally, more educated societies usually receive their improved education levels from the government and, hence, are more apt to defend it.

Finally, in societies where crime is widespread and unchecked, insurgents are more likely to go equally unchecked. When crime becomes rampant and affects the people daily, insurgents attack the governmental legitimacy and strive to demonstrate their own capabilities at preserving the law. Occasionally, insurgents conduct petty crime sprees to foster a perception that the regime has lost control, thereby further undermining the legitimacy of the government and gaining popular support for their cause.

Economic Factors

The human environment that fosters insurgents also includes the economic conditions of the society. When a distinct and large disparity exists between the "haves" and the "have-nots," a perception of interminable inequity that separates the people is more likely. Typically, when the ruling elite wields significant political and economic power, they are heavily influenced by the wealthy. Often the government can be seen as showing undue favoritism to the rich to the detriment of the rest of society. In such cases, insurgents are more likely to easily gain the popular support of the disenchanted masses.

Additionally, as Gurr persuasively articulates, insurgencies are more likely when a perceived discrepancy exists between the conditions of life to which people believe they are entitled and the realization of the goods and conditions which they are capable of acquiring, given the means available to them.[14] It is possible for a segment of a population to have an adequate quality of life and yet still have problems of relative deprivation. The key to understanding relative deprivation is that it is a discrepancy between what society believes it should be capable of achieving and what it actually can achieve. It goes without saying that people are more likely to rebel when they feel they have no other alternatives, a condition more likely when abject poverty exists. Nevertheless, it is possible for a society that has been experiencing moderate improvements in living conditions to grow progressively more militant because of empty promises and unfulfilled hopes, in spite of these improvements.

A high unemployment rate also fosters insurgencies. Unable to find work and suffering lower standards of living, the unemployed are easily recruited by insurgents. In many cases, the causes for unemployment are unrelated to neglect by the government, but disenchanted, destitute people rarely willingly acknowledge governmental efforts when seeking one to blame for their condition. Insurgents often capitalize on these adverse conditions and portray themselves as a suitable alternative to government, capable of solving the people's grievances. Ironically, it is often too late before the people realize that the insurgents were no more capable than the government at solving their woes.

Poor health conditions are also an indicator of larger economic or developmental problems in a country. Statistics including a high infant mortality rate, substandard health care facilities, inadequate water supplies, and high disease rates can point to deeper problems that insurgents use to erode governmental legitimacy and to prop up their cause.

Political Culture and System

One must recognize the importance of the political culture and system in a society. Political culture refers to the relevant and enduring outlook of the people toward politics and government.[15] There are three concepts that characterize the different kinds of citizens in a society: parochials, subjects, and participants.[16] Parochials are those members of society who have little awareness of the political system and little understanding how they can influence it, are predominantly illiterate, and live at the subsistence level. In these sectors, insurgents often have great difficulty mobilizing popular support because parochials are passive and indifferent. Subjects are those citizens who are part of the political system and aware of its impact on their lives, but are not active in it. They can be motivated to support insurgencies if convinced persuasively of the failures of the government, especially when combined with retaliatory governmental oppression. Participants are educated citizens who are not only aware of the political process but are also actively involved in it. They often become the insurgent leadership, especially when their ability to influence the political process is blocked.[17] Additionally, some political cultures and norms exist where centralized control beyond the local or tribal level is resisted. In these cases, insurgencies and governments alike will experience resistance to recruitment of support and are likely to stymie efforts of both sides.

Finally, the political system is acutely important to insurgencies. Some theorists contend that the most effective panacea for insurgency is a genuinely pluralistic democratic policy, where citizens are free to have peaceful paper revolutions via the ballot box every few years. Indeed, Jeff Goodwin and Theda Skocpol assert that, "The ballot box . . . has proven to be the coffin of [many] revolutionary movements."[18] Historical evidence, however, demonstrates that democracy does not guarantee immunity against insurgency. There are often some members of society who simply yearn for power that they cannot obtain within the system. In these cases, insurgents frequently choose to eschew the system and try to work outside it. In most cases, however, truly pluralistic societies have proven surprisingly impervious to insurgencies because of the opportunities that these societies provide to find alternative solutions to their grievances. A common dilemma in Latin America however has been corruption within the regime, which has been especially deleterious to governmental stability. History is replete with examples of governments claiming to represent the best interests of their people but that are fraught with corruption. These regimes are often extremely vulnerable to insurgency.

Analyzing the Insurgents

A Brief History of the Insurgent Group

After gaining an understanding of the country's history and the impact of the physical environment, it is equally important to gain an appreciation for the history of the insurgent group being studied. To set the stage for further evaluation, the first step of this phase of the thesis is to provide general facts, dates, and figures about Sendero.

Insurgency Classification

It is important to understand the seven different kinds of insurgents: anarchists, egalitarians, traditionalists, pluralists, secessionists, reformists, and preservationists to facilitate comparisons between different kinds of insurgencies. O'Neill analyzes the differences in the goals of insurgent groups to help better understand what causes them to develop and succeed. Anarchists seek to eliminate all institutionalized political arrangements because they object to the super-ordinate-subordinate relationship. Egalitarians seek "a new system based on the ultimate value of distributional equality and centrally controlled structure designed to mobilize the people." Traditionalist insurgencies strive "to displace the political system but the values that they articulate are primordial and sacred ones, rooted in ancestral ties and frequently religion; the political structures that they seek to establish are characterized by limited or guided participation and low autonomy." Pluralist groups resist "to establish political communities in which the values of individual freedom, liberty, and compromise are emphasized and in which political structures are differentiated and autonomous." Secessionist organizations "renounce the political community of which they are formally a part . . . and seek to withdraw from it." Reformist factions focus on "the existing allocation of political and material resources, which they consider discriminatory and illegitimate. [They] demand autonomy, not separation." Preservationist insurgents want to maintain the status quo. They generally oppose another existing insurgent faction and "engag[e] in illegal acts of violence against non-ruling groups and authorities trying to effect change."[19]

Insurgency Strategy in Broad Terms

The next step is to determine which strategy the insurgents are using. O'Neill summarizes each of the four distinct major strategies for insurgency: Marxist-Leninist conspiratorial strategy; Mao Tse-tung's strategy of protracted popular war; military-focus strategy of Fidel Castro, Regis Debray and Che Guevara; and urban-warfare strategy of Carlos Marighella.[20] Conspiratorial strategy focuses on a small elite organization seeking to use a low level of swift and decisive violence to decapitate the ruling party, resulting in a coup by either military leaders or elites who are not part of the ruling elite. In this strategy, the insurgent leadership doubts the intellectual or motivational abilities of the masses and believes that they are best suited to lead people to realize what they really need in their government.[21] Protracted popular war strategy uses political means, mass organization, and gradual escalation of violence. Mao's protracted popular war involves three sequential phases, including strategic defensive, strategic stalemate, and strategic offensive. Central to Mao's strategy are the concept of self-reliance and the importance of obtaining extensive popular support.[22] Military-focus strategy centers on the ascendancy of the military arm of revolution and advocates extensive guerrilla or conventional warfare to conduct the campaign.[23] Urban-warfare strategy, common in countries where geographical conditions do not afford insurgents much protection in the rural areas, focuses on an urban-centered strategy in which terrorist attacks play a central role. This strategy advocates the use of smaller organizations that target urban centers and seek to undermine governmental legitimacy by either directly targeting governmental assets or terrorizing the people.[24] O'Neill correctly points out that in the analysis of insurgent strategy classification, one must remember that while most insurgents often adopt one of these strategies or a combination thereof, they do not always adhere to all of their core tenets. Moreover, he points out that insurgent groups can fragment for any number of reasons, and these separate groups may implement conflicting strategies.[25]

Insurgent Organization

In order to understand the factors that drive an insurgent movement or to predict its chances for success, it is critical to understand its organization, ideology, leadership, and structure. A number of factors can cause an insurgency to fail even before it has begun. Organizational or leadership failures can cause an insurgent group to falter before it has the chance to implement a particular strategy or to use the instruments of national power to influence policy or to force regime change. It is essential to describe the insurgent organization, ideology, and leadership separate from their specific strategies.

Ideology

Ideology is often very closely linked to the type of insurgency being fought. At face value, they are typically so completely intertwined that they cannot be separated. For example, an insurgency that espouses communist or Maoist ideals, typically an egalitarian insurgency movement, is so inextricably linked to its communist ideology that compromises may not be possible with a liberal democratic government, and regime change is the only acceptable outcome. Conversely, communist countries, especially during the Cold War era, faced strong pluralistic insurgencies that were so committed to their democratic agenda that there was no compromise possible. When faced with such black-and-white ideological circumstances and when the government represents the antithesis of the ideology of the insurgent group, it is very unlikely that the insurgent group will compromise on its demands. Because the regime in power is facing survival interests and compromises could lead to downfall, it is usually an all-or-nothing circumstance. Those insurgent groups that simply espouse reformist or secessionist objectives may find that some form of compromise is possible.

One additional dilemma that often arises within an insurgency is ideology transformation. Many insurgencies espouse convenient ideologies and goals simply to justify or provide a front for what is essentially a grab for power. It is, therefore, important to recognize the difference between core ideologies and those that are simply used as a means to either gather either popular support of the people through lofty ideals or garner external support from international power brokers or regional adversaries. Determining this is often extremely difficult until years later, after insurgent groups demonstrate that they have no committed allegiance to a specific ideal.

<u>Goals</u>

Understanding an insurgent group's goals is also essential to understanding its chances for success. Much like ideology, goals can be deceptive. Misleading rhetoric, goal conflicts, goal ambiguity, and goal transformation can often make it difficult to ascertain what an insurgency actually wants to achieve.[26] Goal transformation can occur as some insurgents may realize that goals they originally established greatly exceed their capabilities. Conversely, based on weak or disorganized governmental response, they may believe that their goals can expand, as success grows more likely. Goals may also alter as leadership changes. Internal struggles for power may lead to goal conflicts developing into either break-off groups or coups. The likelihood for insurgent success and longevity often is directly proportional to its unity of command, unanimity behind a common goal, and cooperation within the insurgency. Finally, goals can often be couched in grandiose terms seeking to gain popular and external support, but in reality completely misrepresent the true ends of the insurgency. In these circumstances, the truth can be so obscured by rhetoric and propaganda that it is not known until well into the struggle.

Leadership

Leadership is essential to any insurgency. Few insurgent movements can survive the organized and often overpowering technological, economic, and military advantages of the government unless they have strong, focused leadership that can both organize the insurgency and articulate and direct its goals and actions. Ultimately, the primary goal of most insurgencies is to win the hearts and minds of the people, demonstrate the inadequacies of the existing government, and demonstrate their capacity as a suitable replacement for the government to better meet the people's needs. Because insurgencies rarely have sufficient resources and forces to combat governments as equals, they require innovative and competent leadership to lead the insurgency to success.

The leadership of most successful or enduring insurgencies is made up of intellectuals and organizers. Intellectuals are elite, frequently university educated, and typically provide the pivotal leadership for the group on the national level.[27] Intellectuals provide the vision, political direction, and total strategy and are often very charismatic or persuasive. The organizers of an insurgency are those who may not be included in the intellectual elite and may not fully understand the end state for the insurgency, but through the persuasive leadership of the intellectuals have decided to commit their lives to the attainment of the insurgency's goals. These are the military and organizational small unit leaders who take the guidance of the intellectual elites and turn it into executable plans for the overall campaign to be executed by those of the masses who have been converted to the cause. Without leadership at both levels, an insurgency is likely to not only fail but also be quickly eradicated by an organized, concerted effort of the government. Of note when considering leadership, however, is that extremely skilled and charismatic leadership can be a proverbial Achilles' heel for an insurgency, as well as strength. As history has demonstrated periodically, insurgencies that hinge pivotally on the leadership of one key central figure are often quickly and irreversibly undermined or outright destroyed by the capture or elimination of that insurgent leader.

Organization

The physical organization of the insurgency is of key importance to understanding its chances for success in the face of governmental strategies to counter it. O'Neill outlines three structural dimensions with respect to organization: scope, complexity, and cohesion of the insurgent group.[28] "Scope refers to the number and kinds of people across the political spectrum who play either key roles in the movement (political cadres, terrorist, guerrillas, and regular soldiers) or provide active support."[29] The larger the scope of the insurgency, the greater the chance that the insurgency will succeed or endure in the face or governmental opposition. This is the primary objective to the extensive efforts of the insurgency to garner popular support for its cause. Few insurgent leaders are eager to share leadership of the new government, but most view expanding the scope of support for their movement as the best means for extending its life and increasing its chances for victory. Ultimately though, as O'Neill states, "whatever the scope of the insurgency, the effective use of people will depend on the skill of insurgent leaders in identifying, integrating, and coordinating the different tasks and roles essential for success in combat operations, training, logistics, communications, transportation, and the medical, financial, informational, diplomatic, and supervisory areas."[30]

Complexity is the ability of insurgent leaders to coordinate and synchronize the group's efforts.[31] The more complex organizations found in insurgencies often strive to develop parallel hierarchies or shadow governments that take one of several forms. The first is to use the existing government's political and administrative institutions and infiltrate them with insurgent agents to undermine the government at every possible turn and facilitate transition to new leadership when regime change is finally achieved. The second is to develop political and administrative structures that administer, organize, and rule the population in areas controlled by the insurgents.[32] The more robust the organization, the more likely it will survive governmental countermeasures.

Likewise, some insurgencies find that a complex but very compartmentalized organization facilitates its durability in the face of significant governmental opposition, a trend that has become more relevant with the increase of complex transnational terrorist organizations. When an insurgency maintains a focused ideological and supervisory leadership with numerous cells that do not necessarily know what each individual cell is doing, it is far more difficult for governmental counterinsurgency efforts to defeat them. Finally, the complexity of an insurgent group also relates to its development of cells dedicated to employing all of the instruments of national power. This is discussed at greater length when the specific insurgent strategies are addressed in the context of the instruments of national power, but it is important to recognize that when an insurgent group fails to make use of each of these instruments, it will be less likely to succeed.

The final element of organizational structure is cohesion. As O'Neill states, "the absence of unity undermines authoritative control and can create a host of problems for insurgents" and "although the conduct of operations and responsibility may be delegated to local leaders, a general headquarters that exercises authoritative control over policy, discipline, ethics, and ideology is indispensable."[33] He goes on to explain that disunity can undermine insurgent strategy in a number of ways by: (1) undercutting political and military organizational efforts through internecine struggles; (2) leading to conflicting political and military strategies; (3) creating deficiencies by leading competing groups to refuse to share intelligence, logistical supplies, and training abilities; (4) leading to an inability to plan, synchronize, and coordinate complex military operations; (5) diverting personnel and material from attacks on the government to attacks on opposing insurgent factions; (6) undermining external support by leading sympathetic foreign governments to eschew support, believing it would be a wasted effort; (7) facilitating governmental concentration on factions for piecemeal elimination; and (8) leading to a temptation for insurgent factions to provide compromising information to the government about their rivals.³⁴ Without cohesion of organization and objectives, infighting typically results in insurgents working at cross-purposes and facilitates their destruction.

Insurgent Strategy According to the Instruments of National Power

It is the responsibility of a nation's leadership to influence world events in the best interests of its people. In order to achieve national objectives, leaders need power. A nation's ability to achieve its objectives is a product of its application of its available instruments of power. JP 1, *Joint Warfare of the Armed Forces of the United States*, states that: "The United States relies for its security on the complementary application of the basic instruments of national power: diplomatic, economic, informational, and military."³⁵ Other countries and insurgencies are no different. These "represent tangible resources that can be purposefully crafted, manipulated, altered and balanced."³⁶

Generally, when the instruments of national power are discussed, they refer to the means and methods employed by the state to exert its influence or power; however, it is clear that when an insurgency strives to undermine the influence and usurp the authority of a regime, it is most successful when it attempts to do so utilizing the full complement of the instruments of national power. With the exception of rapid and decisive coups that quickly overwhelm the government, most insurgencies that fail to attack the regime utilizing all tools available across the spectrum of diplomatic, informational, military, and economic means are doomed to fail. Initially, most insurgencies start out focusing exclusively on political or military means and graduate to informational and economic strategies. Those that fail to progress to these levels, such as the Tupamoros, are often ephemeral. Naturally, governmental failure to capitalize on these same tools will implement an equally ineffective counterinsurgency strategy and often will perpetuate the insurgency. To be sure, insurgents must often work harder to counter the robust assets available to the regime, especially those that are more entrenched in global organizations and alliances. They nevertheless have the ability, through concerted efforts and strategies, to counter governmental strengths in each of these categories.

<u>Diplomatic</u>

"To participate in the international system, nations communicate with each other."[37] Diplomacy is the art of communicating intentions and exerting, influencing, and building associations with other actors in the international arena. Diplomatic tools most frequently used by states include negotiations, recognition, treaties, and alliances.[38] Insurgent groups have the ability to pursue these tools, much like states do. Insurgencies must garner popular and external support for their cause to legitimize their ideals while undermining the regime. By utilizing tools of diplomacy, insurgencies are able to show their potency to internal and external supporters through formal recognition by alliances or treaties with other international and regional nations or nonstate actors.

For the purposes of this thesis, the diplomatic instrument of national power will focus on the efforts by an insurgency to garner external support for its cause and the use of negotiations with either external and internal actors or the regime itself to achieve its goals, mitigate its weaknesses, or improve its position. O'Neill discusses at length the efforts of insurgents to gain and maintain external support. External support can take on any or all of four different types: moral support, political support, material support, and sanctuary.[39] Through diplomatic negotiations insurgents strike deals with state and non-state actors external to their country to assist them in their cause. Such external support, especially when it evolves from simple moral or political support and recognition to material support and sanctuary, often significantly extends the potency and life of the insurgency. Because overt support for insurgents is often viewed as meddling in the internal affairs of another state, such support is often controversial and may be harder to gain than most insurgents realize, particularly in the aftermath of the Cold War, as state support is on the decline. External support can often go beyond the real material gains or sanctuary that it may provide to the insurgent. Often insurgents desire external support to add to their legitimacy and the populace's perception of their viability as a replacement for the current regime, leading to the next instrument of national power.

Informational

"The power of ideas and information cannot be understated."[40] Insurgents must wage an aggressive information campaign in order to win the hearts and minds of the people and add to the perception not only that their cause is just but also that they represent a better alternative to the existing regime. Governments frequently have the advantage in this area, as they often control or have greater access to the media and means to spread their information campaign. However, insurgents also have access to means to spread their message. Sometimes, they have access to sources that are in insurgent-controlled regions. At other times, their message must be spread by more insidious or subtle means. Many insurgencies in Latin American countries began and have been kept alive in the universities and education centers, touting the right to free expression of ideas as central to the espoused democratic doctrine of the regime while providing tacit or overt support for the militant arm of the insurgents. Insurgents also often use propaganda methods utilizing leaflets or web sources to fight their information campaign. Finally, insurgent leaders often publicize their ideology and spread their message by writing articles or conducting exclusive interviews to help wage their information war. All of these tools are available to insurgents, without which an insurgency is less likely to succeed at winning popular support for its cause.

O'Neill does not specifically address informational instruments of power but discusses efforts to garner popular support extensively. He addresses seven techniques insurgents use to gain this support: charismatic attraction, esoteric appeals, exoteric appeals, terrorism, provocation of governmental repression, demonstrations of potency, and coercion.[41] Charismatic attraction refers to the ability of assertive leaders to demonstrate persuasive leadership skills and the efforts by some insurgent movements to accredit almost supernatural qualities to key leaders to persuade followers to support the movement either actively or passively. Esoteric appeals seek to attract intellectuals by putting the conditions of the insurgent struggle in terms of grandiose ideological or theological struggles. Exoteric appeals concentrate on particular grievances of both the intelligentsia and masses. Terrorism is often employed where esoteric or exoteric appeals fail to garner the desired support. It uses violence or the threat of violence against third parties to demonstrate the government's weakness in the face of the insurgents' strength. Provocation of government repression seeks to get government forces to take reprisals against the masses for crimes and atrocities that the insurgents commit, and uses the reprisals as propaganda to rally support for the insurgents' cause. Insurgents may also attempt to demonstrate their potency by helping the people through material support or the provision of social services that the government has failed to provide. The final method is coercion, which is used to force the people to provide support through intimidation and the threat or actual use of force.[42] Though each of these may employ different instruments of national power, all of them require an application of informational strategies to ensure that insurgent rhetoric does not alienate the masses and undermine insurgent strategies instead of garnering support for their cause.

Military

When one thinks of insurgents, what comes to mind most readily is the military arm. Often the most costly portion of an insurgency's campaign against the regime, the military instrument often receives the most attention by both the insurgent forces and the government. Insurgents may seek external support for their military campaign in the form of training, weapons, advisors, or actual combat forces. This support can come from state actors or other insurgents or terrorists either inside or outside the country. The military of the regime often has both numerical and technological advantages over the insurgents, necessitating unique and unconventional strategies. Under these circumstances, judicious employment of military forces on the asymmetrical battlefield is necessary to counter governmental strengths. Military force may be used to terrorize the masses that do not support the insurgents or can be used to coerce passive or active support from the masses.

Economic

One of the most overlooked instruments of national power, the economic instrument is key to insurgent success. The government uses it to exert its influence abroad and foster prosperity. The tools most frequently used are disincentives, such as trade barriers, embargoes, sanctions, and changes in financial policy that adversely affect target countries, and incentives, such as loans, technology transfers, aid, subsidies, and favorable monetary policies.[43] The tools available to insurgents are less obvious. Insurgents are limited to economic instruments within their liberated regions. In some cases though, as insurgents secure larger portions of liberated areas, they may be able to sell the resources or products within those secured regions to fund their activities.

Insurgents also utilize the economic instrument of power to bribe or extort support from the masses when exoteric appeals fail. Where insurgents strive to supplant the regime, they may use economic incentives to local populations to demonstrate their potency and viability as a suitable replacement for the government. Insurgents may also attempt to provide services such as schools and health clinics to meet the needs of the people and to demonstrate the insurgents' presence and the failure of the government.

In some circumstances, including those in Peru,, extensive amounts of the resources and funding for the insurgent movements come from the sale of narcotics, which provides a greater return for smaller effort. JP 3-07.4, *Joint Counterdrug Operations*, states that: "Much of the world's coca is grown in Peru. . . . Sendero and MRTA are involved in narcotics trafficking in order to help finance their insurgencies. . . . Insurgent groups . . . also benefit from the illicit trade . . . and tax drug profits and protect crops, laboratories, and storage facilities; occasionally they extract payment in weapons."[44] Narcotics trafficking can become so intertwined with an insurgency that to eliminate the insurgents one must first undercut the drug industry. An analysis of insurgency potency and endurance in the face of Peruvian counterinsurgency would be inadequate without an extensive review of the marriage of insurgency and narcotics.

Analyzing the Governmental Response

Governmental Response

O'Neill begins his eighth chapter stating, "Of all the variables that have a bearing on the progress and outcome of insurgencies, none is more important than governmental response."[45] Indubitably an analysis of an insurgency and its chances of success or endurance are incomplete without a thorough analysis of the strategies and methods adopted by the government to counter the insurgents. History is replete with examples of governments that underestimated the potency of an insurgency until it was too late. Governments employ the instruments of national power to exert influence and power internationally and regionally, as well as domestically to combat insurgents.

Governments systematically apply the instruments of national power similarly to insurgents, striving to undermine the insurgent strategies. Governments seek to garner popular and external support much like insurgents to preserve their regime. Their legitimacy and ability to rule is reinforced by every gain in popular support and by fostering international and regional consensus that insurgents within their borders are lawless and power hungry and have no legitimate claim to power in the country. The struggle for power and influence is very much a zero-sum game in which gains by one side necessitate a loss by the other. When governments fail to combat insurgents utilizing every tool at their disposal, insurgencies tend to endure. Additionally, governments are sometimes frustrated in their struggle because the strategies to combat insurgents often require tactics that are antithetical to their ideologies and the promises to their people. Historical examples abound, including Peru, where governments feel compelled to adopt counterinsurgency strategies that contradict the ideals that they claim to represent. In such cases, the inability to stay true to its ideals can often undermine a government, leading to its downfall even in while succeeding in the campaign to defeat the insurgents.

---

[1] Bard E. O'Neill, *Insurgency and Terrorism: Inside Modern Revolutionary Warfare* (McLean, VA: Brassey's Publishing, 1990), ix.

²Ibid., 13-27.

³Ibid., 31-47.

⁴Ibid., 53.

⁵Ibid., 70.

⁶Ibid., 90.

⁷Ibid., 111.

⁸Ibid., 153.

⁹George Santayana, *The Life of Reason* (New York, NY: Charles Scribner's Sons, 1905), 284.

¹⁰O'Neill, 55.

¹¹Ted Robert Gurr, *Why Men Rebel* (Princeton, NJ: Princeton University Press, 1970), 263-264.

¹²O'Neill, 60.

¹³Ibid.

¹⁴Gurr, 13.

¹⁵O'Neill, 63.

¹⁶Gabriel A. Almond and Sidney Verba, *The Civic Culture* (Princeton, NJ: Princeton University Press, 1965), 43.

¹⁷O'Neill, 63-64.

¹⁸Jeff Goodwin and Theda Skopcol. "Explaining Revolutions in the Contemporary Third World," *Politics and Society* 17, no. 4 (December 1989): 495.

¹⁹O'Neill, 17-20.

²⁰Ibid., 32-46.

²¹Ibid., 32-34.

²²Ibid., 34-40.

²³Ibid., 41-44.

²⁴Ibid., 45-47.

²⁵Ibid., 48.

²⁶Ibid., 21-22.

²⁷Ibid., 73-74.

²⁸Ibid., 90-98.

²⁹Ibid., 90.

³⁰Ibid., 91.

³¹Ibid.

³²Ibid., 91-92.

³³Ibid., 98.

³⁴Ibid., 99-101.

³⁵Department of Defense, Director for Operational Plans and Joint Force Development (J-7), Joint Staff, JP 1, *Joint Warfare of the Armed Forces of the United States* (Washington, DC: US Government Printing Office, 14 December 2000), v.

³⁶Ted Davis and Robert Walz, "Power and Theories of International Relations" in *C200: Strategic Studies Readings Book,* C212RA-177-186 (Ft. Leavenworth, KS: USA CGSC, July 2003), 178.

³⁷Ibid., 179.

³⁸Ibid.

³⁹O'Neill, 114-118.

⁴⁰Davis and Walz, 179.

⁴¹O'Neill, 74-75.

⁴²Ibid., 74-84.

⁴³Davis and Walz, 181.

⁴⁴Department of Defense, Director for Operational Plans and Interoperability (J-7), Joint Staff, JP 3-07.4, *Joint Counterdrug Operations* (Washington, DC: US Government Printing Office, 14 February 1998), II-7.

[45]O'Neill, 125.

CHAPTER 4

SETTING THE STAGE FOR THE PERUVIAN CASE STUDY

Historical Context

Peru has a rich, unique heritage and traces its roots back ten thousand years in one of the harshest, most inhospitable environments in the world. Most Peruvians trace their ancestry to the Incas, who created an empire that spanned a third of South America and achieved wealth and cultural sophistication that rivaled and surpassed many empires.

The Incas fought the invading Spaniards in 1532 in one of the most significant clashes between Western and non-Western civilizations in history. The ensuing Spanish conquest, with its fearsome weaponry, use of horses, and ferocity, wiped out the civilized Andean society and created an enormous gulf between victors and vanquished that has forever shaped Peruvian society. Peru's post-conquest, colonial past created a historic separation that foreshadowed the nature of its subsequent problems. Peru became divided economically, socially, and politically between a semi-feudal Native American interior and a more modern, capitalistic, urban, and mestizo or European coast. At the height of Spanish colonialism, a small, wealthy, educated elite dominated the vast majority of Peruvians, subsisting in poverty, isolation, and ignorance. This persistent inequity and the failure of the state to overcome tough economic conditions have prevented economic development and effective integration of the Peruvian nation to this day.

An additional distinctive trait of Peru is the substantial role that outsiders have played in its past. Peru's independence from Spain in 1824 came at the hands of foreigners such as the Venezuelan Simón Bolívar and the Argentine José de San Martín.[1] Independence did little to alter the inequality and underdevelopment in Peru. Self-rule shifted power from the Spanish to the elite *creoles* (South American-born Europeans), which preserved their privileged socioeconomic status. The *creole* elite was either unable or unwilling to change the socioeconomic order to build a viable democratic government.

Foreigners exploited Peru's natural resources, from silver in the colonial period to guano and nitrates in the nineteenth century to copper and oil in the twentieth century, and led Peru's export-dependent economy to be continually manipulated by foreign interests. In 1879 Chile invaded Peru, precipitating the War of the Pacific, resulting in extensive loss of wealth and Peru's nitrate-rich territory.[2] Peruvian history until the 1960s is one of exploitation by ruling elites with military backing, foreign drain of its resources, and numerous personality-based coups as different groups vied for power.

To keep this discussion to those facts relevant to understanding the insurgency in Peru, the following abbreviated analysis is provided. Modern Peruvian history is a tale of numerous oligarchies and only limited democratic tradition. Peruvian political history can be divided into five key periods: consolidation and elite rule (1824-1895); limited civilian democracy (1895-1919); populism and mass parties (1919-1968); reformist military rule (1968-1980); and fully participatory democratic rule (1980-present).[3] Electoral participation was often tied to ownership of land and literacy requirements, and the elite minority and foreign investors owned most of the land until the military agrarian reforms of the 1970s. Despite its democratic tradition, the benefits of democracy did not reach most Peruvians until recently--coincidentally, the same time that the Maoist insurgency Sendero appeared. The causes for this virulent insurgency are complex and have left many seeking answers for its horrific genocide. Using the methodology outlined above, this research explains how the physical and human environments made insurgency likely.

Defining the Environment

The Physical Environment

Terrain

Peru covers 1.285 million square kilometers on the west coast of South America. There were about 17.7 people per square kilometer and fifteen kilometers per policeman in 1992 at the height of Sendero's reign of terror.[4] The Andes run through the country, dividing it into three regions: an arid, dry coastal region--the *costa*; a restrictive and dangerous mountain region--the *sierra*; and the Amazon jungle basin--the *selva* (see figure 2 in appendix A). There is a distinct shortage of arable land, adding to the poor economic potential of much of rural Peru and contributing to the subsistence existence of the rural Indians. Although it has much in the way of natural resources, such as copper, petroleum, timber, fish, iron ore, coal, and natural gas, the poor infrastructure and difficult terrain make most of these difficult to exploit.[5] The closed, restrictive terrain, characteristic of the Upper Huallaga Valley (UHV), provides safe havens and bases for insurgent groups. The Andes, which separate the coastal region from the interior jungle region, have very few developed roads and make it exceedingly difficult for the government to root out the insurgents in their safe havens. These conditions helped the rise of Sendero such that at one point they controlled over one-third of the country, including several entire Peruvian departments, necessitating states of emergency declared by the government to authorize military control and suspension of due process.

Climate

The climate varies from dry in the western coastal desert to temperate in highland valleys. Conditions are harsh and chilly on the western Andean slopes, semi-tropical in the Montaña, and tropical in Amazon Basin. The rainy winter season runs from October through April, with dry summer in remaining months.[6] Other than the harsh conditions of the Andean mountain regions and extensive precipitation in the jungle regions, making it harder for the Army and paramilitary forces to locate insurgents, the climate has limited impact on the insurgency. Generally, the climate provides neither a significant advantage nor disadvantage to the insurgents--certainly not as influential as the topography.

Transportation-Communications Infrastructure

Peru's transportation network is decidedly poor and has deteriorated acutely since the mid-1970s due to poor upkeep in economically tough times. The railroad network totals 1,884 kilometers, and has almost no connections with cities in the interior. A persistent lack of funds for the roads and railroads has led to deterioration and, in some cases, disappearance of Peru's land transport infrastructure. Most of the roads in the Andes are narrow, unimproved, and vulnerable to frequent landslides. Peru's roads in 1990 totaled almost 70,000 kilometers, including about 7,500 paved kilometers, 13,500 gravel kilometers, and 49,000 kilometers of unimproved earthen roads.[7] The majority of the transportation effort goes into sustaining roads in the coastal region and the Pan-American Highway. This poor attention to improving transportation to the interior, particularly in the 1980s, fueled the perception that the government did not care about or provide for the rural population of the *sierra* and *selva*. Additionally, the poor transportation infrastructure made it exceedingly difficult for government forces to react quickly to Sendero's guerilla attacks in the interior (see figure 3 in appendix A).

Peru's telecommunications remain adequate for most needs, but its telephone system in 1990 was one of the least developed in Latin America. With an abundance of

AM radio stations and 140 television stations, its information network remained generally adequate for its state of development. Communications infrastructure remained lacking in the interior, making it difficult for the government to deliver its message to the rural population.[8] The inadequate transportation network and coastal oriented communications decidedly favored the guerillas. In the early 1990s, when the Fujimori government made efforts to correct these deficiencies with Army-sponsored road projects, Sendero countered by targeting and destroying bridges linking the Huallaga Valley to Lima and killed development workers as a strategy to isolate the coca farmers and rural peasants (known as *campesinos*) to make them dependent on Sendero.[9]

The Human Environment

Demographic Distribution

Peru is a complex amalgam of ancient and modern cultures, populations, conflicts, and dilemmas. The population, 28.4 million in 2003, is one of the most heterogeneous societies in Latin America.[10] The ethnic composition of Peru is as follows: a very small minority of European, about 15-percent of the population, which has held exclusive power throughout most of Peruvian history; the mestizos, making up the majority of the coastal and urban population, totaling 37-percent; Blacks, Japanese, Chinese, and others, making up 3-percent; and the Amerindians, largely Quechua or Aymara-speaking, making up the remaining 45-percent and residing predominantly in the underdeveloped shantytowns, or *pueblos jóvenes,* surrounding Lima and the other metropolises, or in the rural and underdeveloped interior.[11]

Internal demographic changes since the 1950s have shaped contemporary Peru in fundamental ways. The population has tripled in four decades.[12] With this population boom came a major migration from the interior to the urban areas in search of paying jobs (see tables 1 and 2 in appendix B). Many migrants left the interior hoping for better living conditions in the cities, swelling the cities by 500-percent.[13] Those living in the slums and the interior supplied a sizable estranged populace for Sendero recruitment.

These demographic transformations in the second half of the twentieth century led anthropologist José Matos Mar to describe the 1980s "as a great *desborde popular* (overflowing of the masses)."[14] Once dominated by *creole* minorities, Lima became increasingly overwhelmed with people from the interior. Urbanization and *desborde popular* tended to overwhelm the capacity of a state, already substandard in its performance, to deliver even the most basic governmental services to the vast majority of the population, thus fostering reasons for Sendero to eventually urbanize its strategy.

Social Structure

Organized social groups have played less of a role in Peru than in any other Latin American country. Personalized governments organized more on the leadership of a single leader than on allegiance to a party or ideology have characterized Peruvian politics for centuries. A long history in governments who favored foreign investment and elite concerns led to very little support for popular organizations until the return to democratic rule in 1980 and facilitated an environment ripe for insurgency.

Historical Proclivity for Violence

A tradition of turning to violence to solve problems can foster insurgency. Resorting to extraordinarily violent means, Sendero succeeded for over twelve years in challenging the authority of the state, particularly in the more remote areas of the interior, where the presence of the state has always been tenuous. Violence has been a common theme throughout Andean history, including Incan expansion, the Spanish conquest and colonialism, countless Native American insurrections and the resultant suppression, the struggle for independence in the 1820s, and the devastating War of the Pacific with Chile in 1879. The nineteenth century was marked by violence in the transfer of power, as Peru had over fifteen constitutions in its first forty years. Of thirty-five presidents, only four were elected according to constitutional procedures--most came to power by coup.[15] The twentieth century did not see much improvement, as most transfers of power resulted from either violence and assassinations or coercion through the threat of force.

Insurgency was not a new phenomenon in Peru with the emergence of Sendero in 1980. Efforts to force land reform in Cusco Department in the 1950s frequently resulted in violent clashes between landowners, the military, the police, and farmers. In spite of ruthless suppression by the military in most cases, the government relented and began a modest land redistribution that inspired many others around the Peruvian highlands to carry out their own forced land occupations. More radical groups, inspired by the Cuban revolution, saw the growing rural ferment as an opportunity to begin armed revolution in the countryside. Several such organizations included the Movimiento de la Izquierda Revolucionaria, created in 1962, which was effectively destroyed in 1965; the Guillermo Lobatón's Túpac Amaru, which was also destroyed in Junín in January 1966 after six months of skirmishes; and the Ejército de la Liberación Nacional, a Castroite force founded in 1962, defeated in early 1966 in Ayacucho.[16] These guerrilla activities and military responses demonstrate that there is decidedly a historical proclivity in Peru to resort to violence as the most effective means for resolving differences and, in the case of the government, to ruthlessly suppress dissent.

Class System and Ethnic Discrimination

In some societies, class distinctions and associated discrimination develop along economic or religious lines. For Peru, the divisiveness has always been based first on ethnic or racial lines, leading to economic stratification; therefore, both class systems and ethnic discrimination will be addressed together here.

Like other Latin American cultures, Peruvian culture has developed distinct cleavages and classes as a result of ethnic and linguistic differences. Though the majority of the population was and is Amerindian, this segment has always been regarded as the lower class. Mestizos, mulattos, and Asian immigrants typically fall somewhere in between, forming the middle class and upper end of the lower class. European descendants, the descendents of conquerors, have always been regarded as the upper class. The geographical location of these different peoples has reinforced this. For the first 150 years of Peruvian history, clear divisions could be found based on the locale of the separate classes: the upper-class in the urban, more affluent cities; the middle class in the outskirts of the larger cities and throughout the smaller cities of the coastal region; and the lower class remaining in the underdeveloped interior.

In recent times, exemplified by Alberto Fujimori's rise to power in 1990, Japanese and Chinese immigrants have been able to achieve a higher degree of social mobility that has long been impossible for the natives. Ethnic discrimination against the natives is a large part of this. In colonial times, the native inhabitants were known collectively as savages (*chunchos*) and in formal documents they were somewhat more tactfully referred to as jungle people (*selvícolas* or *selváticos*). Regarded as wild and dangerous, they were considered simple, lazy, and useless people who were frequently obstructions to the path of progress.[17] The word *indio* holds strong negative meaning to most whites and mestizos.[18] The stigma is so strong to this day that natives who want to escape their lesser social status feel compelled to change their identity and are expected to learn Spanish and deny their Quechua roots.[19] Ethno-racial attributes still affect social class. A Native American might become fluent in Spanish, earn a university degree, and become wealthy, but would still be considered an *indio* and an unacceptable associate. Yet, opportunities exist for social mobility as a mestizo or a foreigner, or especially if one is white.[20] These circumstances, deep-seated in Peruvian society, have frustrated any efforts at pursuing a Peruvian unity through nationalism, and help to cultivate insurgency.

Levels of Education

In Peru, education is regarded as indispensable to personal advancement. In 1988, there were over 27,600 primary schools in Peru, one for virtually every hamlet with over 200 persons throughout the country.[21] Unfortunately there were only 5,400 secondary schools, making basic education available to all, but higher education far more difficult to obtain.[22] Nevertheless, for most Indians the village school is the most important first step to escape their abject poverty and the historical ethnic and racial discrimination.

Reforms during the *docenio* (the twelve-year rule of the military from 1968 to 1980) significantly expanded educational opportunities, and the neglected Indians began to be educated. Through schooling, many Indians were able to learn Spanish, the first step to being accepted in society, and were actively encouraged to discard their Native American heritage and language. This education both fostered and countered the propensity for insurgency. On one hand, when available, education provided a better standard of living for many and helped them to assimilate, in spite of continued racial prejudices, into mainstream Peruvian society. These opportunities helped to counter the claims of instigators and insurgent leaders in the 1980s that the government had neglected the Indian people. Conversely, the absolute dearth of educational opportunities in the first 130 years of Peruvian history for the Indian people kept the majority of them ignorant of what life could be like and what options to seek change might include. This contributed to the lack of viable insurgencies from within the neglected interior for much of Peruvian history. Additionally, while schooling began to improve the educational levels of many Native Americans, including by the 1980s more representation in secondary schooling and universities, this did not coincide with improvements in options to gain a share of the wealth of society, resulting in more educated but disaffected people.

In 1960 Peru had only five universities with 30,000 students. By 1992 there were forty-six universities with close to 500,000 students. Unfortunately, due to economic stagnation, the majority of these students knew that they were candidates for some kind of underemployment, which fed resentment.[23] Insurgent leaders commonly come from university intellectual elites, and many leaders of Peru's radical groups taught and recruited through the universities. The lack of widespread education in the 1960s contributed to the failed insurgencies of that period, but expanded education and an increased awakening to unfulfilled dreams in the 1970s facilitated insurgency by 1980.

Levels of Crime

Insurgents, attacking governmental legitimacy, often point to high crime levels as indices of government failure. Despite the return to civilian government in 1980 and the widespread hope that this would normalize the judiciary, this was not the case. Economic decline in the 1980s prevented providing the judicial branch with the necessary funds and contributed to increasing crime rates as more resorted to crime to cope with rising unemployment.[24] Insurgent coercion and assassinations of judicial officials left many vacancies in the system, crippling law enforcement. By the late 1980s the economic crises, the insurgency, and the drug trafficking were all interconnected. Drug trafficking crimes recorded by the Peruvian police between 1980 and 1986 increased by 67-percent, almost four times the rate of crime overall. Insurgency and drug-related cases tied up the courts and left 80-percent of the incarcerated prisoners waiting for a long time to be tried; even worse, nearly 10-percent had completed their sentences but remained in jail.[25] Thousands of extra-judicial disappearances and human rights violations occurred during the 1980s, most linked to the Army and police in the emergency zones. This environment led to erosion of governmental legitimacy and increased support for insurgencies.

Economic Factors

Disparity between Haves and Have-Nots

There has always been a distinct difference between the haves and the have-nots in the Peruvian economy (see table 3 in appendix B). Two-thirds of Peruvians by 1990 lived in abject poverty.[26] A large migration of Peruvians from the rural Andean regions to the coastal urban areas led to significant overpopulation, exceeding governmental ability to provide for its citizens. In 1992, the capital city of Lima, plagued by an inadequate urban infrastructure, had over six million inhabitants, with two-thirds living in abysmal conditions (more than two million had no water or drainage in their huts and two million lived in cramped inner-city slums).[27] The conditions were worse for those living in rural areas. In fact, real wages for Peruvians plummeted in the 1980s such that average wage levels in 1989 were 52-percent below those of 1970.[28] Poor economic policy in the 1970s and 1980s, and extensive mortgaging of Peru's future with huge foreign debt led Peru into the worst economic crisis since the 1879 war with Chile.[29] This disparity in wealth between the elites and the rest of Peru made conditions ripe for insurgency.

Relative Deprivation

Unlike the historical trend of military regimes in Latin American history, the 1968 coup by General Juan Velasco Alvarado was decidedly reformist and was not designed to preserve the power of the elites. Beginning the *docenio* with commitments to foster "national pride, social solidarity, the end of dependency, a worker-managed economy, and fully participatory democracy," the military soon found that it was failing because it had tried to do too much.[30] Most assessments of the military regime deduce that military leaders erred in seeking to reform more than the economy could support. "In attempting to do too much, government resources were stretched too thin and the quality of delivery suffered at the same time as public expectations were being raised."[31] In this case, it appears that it is better to make no promises at all than to make promises and not deliver.

The record of the democratic governments of the 1980s and early 1990s is not much better in this respect. Although these governments hoped to provide for the people, conditions grew progressively worse as a result of poor political and economic policies and harsh economic downturns. Elected presidents failed repeatedly to deliver on promises, leading most citizens to be completely disenchanted with the hollow promises of their leaders. Although improvements were made, they did not benefit the entire population. In 1992, much of the interior remained backward and was characterized by massive unemployment, lack of hygiene, and poverty. While Peruvians may be more conscious of their rights, "their expectations have been frustrated as a consequence of lack of work and social mobility."[32] With the partial improvements in societal conditions and an increased awareness of what the government should provide, Peruvians experienced a stark contrast between what they feel they were entitled to and what they could actually achieve. "Peru's socioeconomic and political disarray has taken on its present pattern after . . . incessant promises of development, jobs, and progress without fulfillment."[33] As discussed in chapter 3, this relative deprivation feeds insurgency.

Unemployment

Making conditions worse, Peru's population tripled in only four decades, without an equal growth in the economy. In fact, by the late 1980s severe inflation, loss of foreign markets, and loss of funds from international aid and bank agencies resulted in a significant downturn in the already poor economy. President García's government sought to control the floundering economy by slowing payment of international debt to no more than 10-percent of all Peruvian exports. This action, however, shattered the hope of the international community that Peru's economy could rebound, and virtually dried up the chances for additional loans as two-thirds of Peru's current loans were in arrears by 1990.

Continuing the downward spiral, Peru's gross domestic product declined by 30-percent in the late 1980s and inflation was 7,650-percent in 1990.[34] Hyperinflation of a combined 2,500,000-percent between 1986 and 1992 pushed the majority into abject poverty.[35] This stagnation led to rampant unemployment and fed the growing insurgency movement with the unemployed. Unemployment rates during the 1980s and in the early 1990s ebbed and flowed between 50-to-80-percent and about 63-percent of the population lived below the poverty line, leading to a large number of unemployed or underemployed discontents eager to see changes and primed for insurgent recruitment.[36]

Poor Health Conditions

A review of health statistics amply illustrates Peru's vulnerability to disease and the uneven distribution of resources to combat it (see table 4 in appendix B). In 1990 the majority of the best health facilities were concentrated in metropolitan Lima and other larger coastal cities. The disparity between coastal urban facilities and interior rural facilities remained stark. The doctor-to-citizen ratio in Lima in 1990 was 400:1 and in the interior a horrible 12,000:1. Ratios were similar with respect to hospital beds, nurses, and medical specialties.[37] Potable water was sparse in the cities and virtually absent in rural areas leading to a wide variety of waterborne diseases. The leading causes of death included respiratory infections, common colds, malaria, tuberculosis, influenza, and measles. Although Peru's infant mortality rate dropped from 130 to 80 per 1,000 births between 1965 and 1991, the rate in 1991 was still double that of Colombia and four times the rate of Chile.[38] The segment of the population that suffered most was predictably the interior, providing more justification for insurgent claims of governmental impotency.

Political Culture and System

Electoral policy was extremely restrictive for much of Peruvian history. Spanish colonial rule was very authoritarian and mercantilist, providing little opportunity for self-rule. Though allegedly democratic, Peru has an awful track record in true democratic ideals. Independence brought little improvement to the masses and only perpetuated elite rule, with very self-interested policies as the norm. It was not until 1872 that the first civilian president was elected, though only by a small group of elites who were allowed to vote.[39] From 1824 until 1931, only literate, land-owning males were allowed to vote. In 1931, middle-class citizens were included as land ownership requirements were relaxed. Women did not receive the right to vote until 1956 and literacy requirements excluded the majority of the Quechua-speaking people until the constitution of 1978 instituted universal suffrage.[40] The exclusion of this large percentage of the population for so long predictably fostered an environment suitable for insurgency; it is surprising that an insurgency did not develop significantly prior to 1980.

With long-standing traditions of exclusive governance and favoritism for select minorities, another political and cultural trend formed as political corruption became commonplace. Elitist, opportunistic governments in the nineteenth century were rife with corruption and favoritism. Foreign entrepreneurship lined the pockets of most of the ruling class. Conditions in the twentieth century did not improve much. From 1919 to 1968, whether ruled by the military or civilian oligarchy, political organizations were discouraged and loyalty to the person in power was encouraged by "favored treatment for the elites and distribution of jobs, and services to politically aware non-elite segments."[41] With the rise of military reformists in 1968, corruption waned somewhat as leaders tried to expand opportunities and land reform, but overaggressive commitments to reform led to the collapse of this reformist government and a call in 1978 to return to civilian rule.

With the return to democracy, many saw opportunity and hope for a better Peru. From 1980 to 1985, democracy floundered under Fernando Belaúnde, who had spent the *docenio* in exile and was out of touch with Peru's political realities. Alan García Pérez experienced brief initial success but soon led Peru into devastating economic conditions with an abysmal economic policy. Worsening the situation, several corruption scandals involving APRA were uncovered. The atmosphere of chaos, a failing economy, and the governmental and judicial corruption discredited state institutions and political parties.[42]

Corruption went beyond the presidency and extended throughout the entire political system. In many cases, politicians who sought to rectify the imbalances between the classes of Peruvian society, counter the virulent insurgency, and lead Peru to a better quality of life were stymied by rampant corruption. The Peruvian drug epidemic, centered on coca production, also fostered corruption throughout the government.[43] Due to national economic recession in the late 1980s, García instituted severe pay cuts for most government workers and downsized many departments. At a time when drug trafficking and Sendero were running rampant, these cutbacks significantly increased the potential for corruption. When top Army generals make only $400 a month and supreme court judges about $300 to $400 per month, temptations can be difficult to resist.[44]

The judiciary was severely corrupted, suffering from "incompetence, slowness, absurd decisions, corruption, politicization, and vulnerability to intimidation."[45] In the 1980s, bribes to determine judicial venues, improve prison conditions, or acquit captured insurgents were common. For years, several Peruvian prisons were completely controlled internally by prisoners held for terrorism and the courts blocked the return of police control. Occasionally, judges freed prominent Sendero leaders long before the completion of their sentences for "good behavior" while many of the country's petty criminals from the poorest strata languished in prison for years before even receiving a trial.[46]

Before April 1992, the Peruvian legislature (the Congress) consisted of delegates of at least ten parties who formed unstable coalitions of convenience, only to have them repeatedly collapse due to the personal ambitions of their leaders. During these dire times, with all others taking pay cuts and governmental downsizing, Congress voted for "large salary increases and bigger staffs while [it] paid a pittance to its soldiers."[47]

Discussed more extensively below, corruption crippled efforts by the president to cure the ills of Peru at every turn. Even when opposing parties ran on similar campaign platforms and purportedly advocated the desired changes, personal ambition frequently blocked any kind of resolution.[48] Suspicions also mounted that insurgents paid politicians to block internationalization of the Peruvian problem. The corruption was so bad that on 5 April 1992 Alberto Fujimori suspended the constitution, dissolved the elected Congress, purged the judiciary, and, with military backing, assumed complete power.[49]

This analysis of Peruvian history and the physical and human environment sheds light on why Peru was ripe for insurgency. The physical environment is harsh; economic neglect and mismanagement of the interior and Peruvian economy as a whole led to inadequate transportation-communication infrastructure and underdevelopment in the country. Distinct disparities between social and economic classes along ethnic lines with deep-rooted prejudices, ensuing economic inequities among these classes linked to mismatched educational opportunities and health services, among other governmental services, have made it surprising that virulent insurgencies did not form sooner. The state, in spite of itself, often contributed to setting the conditions for insurgency with rampant corruption within the state institutions, unchecked crime rates, and the failure of many politicians to deliver on promises. These factors raised expectations above capabilities and led to relative deprivation. The next step is to analyze the insurgency that formed to better understand its context in this environment.

---

[1]David P. Werlich, *Peru: A Short History* (Carbondale and Edwardsville, IL: Southern Illinois University Press, 1978), 62-65.

[2]Ibid.,106-108.

[3] David Scott Palmer, "Peru: Democratic Interlude, Authoritarian Heritage, Uncertain Future," 258-282, in *Latin American Politics and Development*. 3d ed., ed. Howard J. Wiarda and Harvey F. Kline (Boulder, CO: Westview Press, Inc., 1990), 261.

[4] Rex A. Hudson, *Peru: A Country Study* (Washington, D.C.: Library of Congress Press, 1993), 63.

[5] Ibid., 142-143.

[6] Ibid., xvi.

[7] Ibid., 163.

[8] Ibid., 164.

[9] Bernard W. Aronson, "Peru's Brutal Insurgency: Sendero Luminoso," *US Department of State Dispatch* 3, no. 12 (23 March 1992): 239.

[10] Central Intelligence Agency. World Fact Book Country Studies: Peru, 18 December 2003; [database on-line] available from http://www.cia.gov/cia/publications/factbook/geos/pe.html; Internet; accessed on 11 January 2004.

[11] Hudson, 95.

[12] Miguel Esperanza, "Terrorism in Peru," *America* 166, no. 21 (20 June 1992): 537.

[13] Ibid.

[14] Hudson, 4.

[15] Palmer, "Peru: Democratic Interlude," 262.

[16] Hudson, 304.

[17] Ibid., 96.

[18] Ibid., 100.

[19] Ibid.

[20] Ibid., 100.

[21] Ibid., 127.

[22] Ibid., 130.

[23] Esperanza, 538.

[24] Hudson, 311.

[25] Ibid., 311.

[26] Aronson, 238.

[27] Esperanza, 537.

[28] Palmer, "Peru: Democratic Interlude," 278.

[29] Ibid., 280.

[30] Ibid., 266.

[31] Ibid., 280.

[32] Esperanza, 538.

[33] Hudson, 125.

[34] David Scott Palmer, "Peru, the Drug Business and Shining Path: Between Scylla and Charybdis," *Journal of Interamerican Studies and World Affairs* 34, no. 3 (fall 1992): 65.

[35] Michael Radu, "Can Fujimori Save Peru?" *Bulletin of the Atomic Scientists* 48, no. 6 (July/August 1992): 16.

[36] Palmer, "Peru, the Drug Business and Shining Path," 65.

[37] Hudson, 133.

[38] Ibid., 133.

[39] Palmer, "Peru: Democratic Interlude," 260.

[40] Ibid., 271.

[41] Ibid., 264.

[42] Hudson, 244.

[43] Radu, 19.

[44] James S. Torrens, "Eyes Open in Peru," *America* 172, no. 9 (13 March 1995): 4.

[45] Radu, 20.

[46] Ibid.

[47] Ibid., 17.

[48] Ibid., 20.

[49] Ibid.

CHAPTER 5

INSURGENTS AND THE GOVERNMENT

<u>Analyzing the Insurgents</u>

A Brief History of Sendero

Two insurgencies were the focus of Peruvian counterinsurgency efforts for the last twenty years. The first was the Movimiento Revolucionario Túpac Amaru (MRTA), founded in 1984 by Victor Polay Campos.[1] MRTA remained relatively small and fought through the late 1980s until Polay was captured in 1987 and jailed on murder and drug trafficking charges. In 1990, following a mass jailbreak of forty-seven MRTA prisoners, Polay escaped but was recaptured in July 1992. MRTA dwindled in importance until its brief bid for power in seizing the Japanese ambassador's residence in December 1996. After its defeat there, MRTA effectively disappeared.[2]

The second insurgency group and focus of this thesis is Sendero. During the *docenio*, a number of diverse political parties began to form, one of which was the Communist Party of Ayacucho (see figure 4 in appendix A). This party evolved into the Communist Party of Peru on the Shining Path of José Carlos Mariátegui or simply "Shining Path," translated as *Sendero Luminoso*. Sendero quickly transformed into the most ruthless insurgency movement in Latin America.

Sendero traces its origins to the writings of José Carlos Mariátegui, a radical Peruvian journalist from the 1930s, whose interpretation of Marxism-Leninism inspired the formation of the Peruvian Socialist Party, which evolved into the Peruvian Communist Party (PCP).[3] Infighting and personal rivalries led to numerous splits within the PCP, and schisms ensuing from the Sino-Soviet split resulted in the emergence of

Sendero, one of the most extreme factions. One of the key issues causing these rifts centered on different "interpretations of Peru's relative stage of development, the party's relationship vis-à-vis the government, and the role of violence."[4] Sendero's position was that armed struggle was the only means for coming to power and that the party should have nothing to do with the illegitimate government except to destroy it. The movement was founded by Abimaél Guzmán, who was a professor of philosophy at the University of San Cristobal de Huamanga (UNSCH) in Ayacucho.[5]

Sendero began as a little-known political movement in the mid-1970s, and focused on forming its goals and garnering popular support. Sendero's first violent act was to burn the ballot boxes in the Ayacucho village of Chuschi on the eve of Peru's 1980 presidential election, protesting the return of democracy to Peru after twelve years of military oligarchy.[6] Since then and until Guzmán's capture in 1992, Sendero waged an unrelenting war on both the Peruvian government and any who sought to alleviate the suffering of the Peruvian people, including international aid organizations, UN workers, Peruvian and foreign industry workers and leaders, and even religious leaders.

The exact figures for the toll inflicted on Peruvian society in the twelve plus years of struggle with Sendero are unclear, but the most consistent figures cite more than 23,000 deaths and in excess of twenty billion dollars in damages.[7] Such raw data are impersonal and misleading to the true nature of this insurgency. To understand the truly horrific viciousness of Sendero, it is necessary to recount some of their more sadistic activities. Each of the following were described by Bernard Aronson, the Assistant Secretary for Inter-American Affairs, in his testimony before the Subcommittee on Western Hemisphere Affairs of the House Foreign Affairs Committee on 12 March 1992.

In January 1990, a Sendero group, mostly children under sixteen, shot two French tourists they took off a bus passing through a rural area. The youngest member of the group was forced to beat one of the victim's skulls with a large rock until it was completely crushed--an initiation rite. In May 1991, Sendero terrorists publicly shot to death an Australian nun, Sister Irene McCormick, of the Catholic relief organization Caritas, who worked to help Peru's poor in Junín. Her body was left lying where it fell for twenty-four hours on orders from Sendero. On 15 February 1992, María Elena Moyano, Vice Mayor of Villa El Salvador, Lima's largest shantytown, was shot at point-blank range and killed after leaving a barbecue with her family. A dynamite charge was then thrown on her body, scattering her remains more than one hundred yards, all in view of her family. She was targeted because of her efforts to reform the political system and help the poor in overt resistance to Sendero's aims. A Catholic priest from Ayacucho told of ritual murders of peasants who refused to cooperate or tried to escape Sendero during its early years. In one case, a "people's trial" was held and those convicted by the Sendero terrorists were punished by being stripped and tied to a post in the town square, after which every person in the town--men, women, and children--was forced to cut a piece of flesh from the living body; this torture went on for as long as an hour until the victims died from shock and loss of blood.[8] Descriptions of torture include executions of fathers and mothers while their children were forced to watch, children tortured to coerce parents to commit crimes for Sendero or to demonstrate loyalty, and even "children forced to eat their parents' tongues."[9] Even more shocking are accounts of a most horrific Sendero tactic used to attack a major Lima hotel using a *ninobomba*, when a child is strapped with dynamite and exploded as he walks near the target--all for the good of the cause.¹⁰ Such ruthless tactics were not just typical at the height of their terrorism in the early 1990s, but also characterized their methods for quite some time.

Several accounts compare Sendero's reign of terror to that of the Pol Pot's Khmer Rouge in Cambodia. Pol Pot, in a genocidal cleansing of his own people to eliminate opposition to his regime, murdered in excess of 1.7 million Cambodians. Many people believe that had the Fujimori government in the mid-1990s not effectively destroyed Sendero, Guzmán and Sendero would have been well on their way to a similar horrific death toll in the name of pursuing pure communism. Indeed, Guzmán said in a rare interview in 1985 that "violence is a universal law with no exception" and "in order to annihilate the enemy and preserve one's forces, we have to pay a war cost, a blood cost, the need of sacrificing one part for the sake of triumph of the people's war."¹¹ In fact, in November 1991, Luis Arce Borja, Sendero's European representative and editor of Sendero's periodical *El Diario*, told a Lima newspaper that the second stage of the war--strategic equilibrium--would cost one million Peruvian lives.¹² Fortunately for Peru, Guzmán was captured on 12 September 1992 by an elite unit of the National Directorate Against Terrorism that raided a residence in the middle-class neighborhood of Surco.¹³ What remained of Sendero after Guzmán's capture dissipated in 1994 after Guzmán "offered peace terms" from his jail cell in January of 1994.¹⁴

Insurgency Classification

To classify Sendero into one of O'Neill's types of insurgency is somewhat difficult. Sendero has always been very secretive and closed off. At first, its practice of eradicating all institutions of authority and its competition with any institutions that might seek to alleviate the suffering of the Peruvian people indicated that Sendero is anarchistic.

After further analysis, however, it is clear that this strategy is merely a facet of its overall stratagem to precipitate a complete uprising of the Peruvian masses to overthrow the democratic government. Sendero's goals are most consistent with those of an egalitarian insurgency because of its hope to impose "a new system based on the ultimate value of distributional equality and centrally controlled structure designed to mobilize the people and radically transform the social structure within [the] existing political community."[15] In some ways, one could claim that Sendero was traditionalist in nature, but in actuality its early use of traditionalism and ancient culture was merely a means to the end of swaying the Amerindians to their cause. At its core, Sendero's brand of communism is a mix of Marx, Lenin, and Mao with modifications shaped by the self-proclaimed fourth sword of Marxism, Abimaél Guzmán. By analyzing Guzmán's few interviews and the undercurrents of *El Diario*, Sendero's newspaper, one can better understand Sendero's plan to win its revolution to achieve pure communism by crossing a river of blood.

Insurgency Strategy in Broad Terms

Sendero's undisputed leader is Guzmán, who was deeply influenced by Chinese communism while living in China during the Cultural Revolution. He has always brought a strong Maoist orientation to Sendero, focused on a strategy of rural, peasant-based revolution through a long protracted popular war. Ideologically, Sendero is extremely rigid. However, the facts demonstrate that over time Sendero has proven flexible in its strategy to win the people's revolution. In broad terms, Guzmán felt that Mao's three-phased strategy of protracted popular war required some modification as he developed a five-phased process designed for the unique circumstances of Peru's situation: (1) to convert the backward areas into advanced and solid bases of revolutionary support; (2) to attack the symbols of the bourgeois state and of revisionist elements; (3) to generalize violence and develop guerrilla warfare; (4) to conquer and expand bases of support; and (5) to lay siege to the cities and bring about the total collapse of the state.[16]

Contrary to Mao's precepts, Guzmán did not come from the rural peasantry nor did most of Sendero's leadership throughout their twelve-year reign of terror. After some initial successes in the early 1980s, popular support among the rural peasantry, the purported beneficiaries of the people's war, was very difficult for Guzmán to maintain. As will be discussed at length later, Sendero's ability to garner popular support among the *campesinos* was frequently tied to intimidation and coercion and less to ideological affinity. Their inability to follow through in mobilizing the rural population due to conflicts with Sendero's dogmatic adherence to revolutionary violence led some analysts, such as William Hazleton and Sandra Woy-Hazleton, to describe Sendero's strategy as more in line with Marxist-Leninist conspiratorial strategy.[17] Sendero, however, has predominantly claimed to be fighting a unique version of Mao's protracted popular war.

Governmental success in the mid 1980s led Sendero to hold its first plenary session in September of 1987, at which time Sendero's leaders reviewed the status of the people's war and "endorsed a strategic shift from protracted rural warfare to an accelerated, urban-based revolution."[18] Beginning in 1988, a noticeable increase in insurgent activity in the major cities, especially in Lima and the *pueblos jóvenes*, demonstrated Sendero's shift from purely rural warfare to one synthesizing ideas from Marighella's urban-warfare strategy, while sustaining a concurrent rural base. Evidently, Sendero's strategy has been anything but rigid. It has metastasized over time, seeking to adapt new strategies to win its people's war while adhering to its core principle of the imperative of revolutionary violence to cleanse Peru of its corruption. Further analysis of Sendero's ideology helps to demonstrate its doctrinaire and revolutionary dogma.

Insurgent Organization

Ideology

The role of ideology has long been considered one of the most critical issues in any revolutionary movement--it can be what draws the people to forsake the existing government and flock to the revolutionary cause. As discussed in chapter 3, some insurgencies change their ideology as a matter of convenience when it suits their purposes. Sendero, however, is not one of those insurgencies. It has dogmatically stuck to a single ideological platform since it began the people's war in 1980. In fact, Sendero's ideology dates back earlier to when Abimaél Guzmán first formulated his radical ideas in the late 1960s as a professor of philosophy, and has remained unchanged since.

Sendero's ideology is unequivocally communism--in fact, according to the Party, a pure form of communism unlike that of any other communists. Guzmán's ideas have been described as "a mix of Gang of Four-Cultural Revolution Maoism, Cambodia's Pol Pot, some ideas freely adopted from José Carlos Mariátegui, and Incan mysticism and nationalism."[19] No one who studies Sendero's ideology, though, could confuse it with the modern communism found in China or Cuba. In fact, Sendero firmly believes that Sendero is the "last bastion of true communism in the world," that Castro is a revisionist lackey of the US, and that "capitalist-imperialist dogs" now govern China.[20] Unlike most communist insurgencies, according to testimony before the House Foreign Affairs Committee, "only Sendero saw the fall of the Eastern communist governments as a positive step where the people overthrew decadent bourgeois communism to make way for pure communism."[21] Sendero's ideology proclaims that violence is a universal law with no exceptions because it is the only way to replace the bourgeois oppressive class with the proletariat. Indeed, in 1988, in an interview with *El Diario*, Guzmán proclaimed that Peru was totally corrupt, that the bourgeois government was incapable of changing it, and that Sendero remained committed to destroying the existing order by exacting *la cuota*, the blood cost, the necessary sacrifice for the triumph of the people's war.[22]

A well-known characteristic of Sendero's ideology is its rigidity and unrelenting refusal to compromise or cooperate with other leftist movements in Peru. In some cases, a doctrinaire ideology such as Sendero's could prove useful to help foster feelings of solidarity. Alternatively though, such rigidity can also dissuade the participation of those who do not understand or agree with their particular breed of extremism. Sendero's ideological rigidity tended to alienate many of its would-be *campesino* followers. Many of the peasants simply wanted a better way of life and not necessarily to be active participants in the revolutionary bloodbath. Sendero, however, could not abide an apolitical peasantry. When their ideology did not win over the people, Sendero resorted to coercive violence to mobilize them. For twelve years, the peasants for whom Sendero was purportedly fighting suffered most at the hands of Sendero violence. Consequently, Sendero's ideological rigidity soon proved more detrimental than beneficial.

Goals

Sendero's goals are clear and have remained remarkably unchanged throughout its campaign of violence. In the cases of some insurgencies, goals begin small and are expanded, but Sendero's objectives began big and remained big. According to Sendero's proselytizing, the goal of the people's war was to establish a "New Democratic Republic, a joint dictatorship of the proletariat, peasantry and petit bourgeoisie" and to transform Peruvian society from "semi-feudal, bureaucratic capitalism" to pure and true communism.[23] They were to accomplish this by exploiting social and economic tensions and by exacerbating the suffering of the Peruvian masses. Some revolutionary movements also see transformations in their goals as leadership changes hands, but Sendero has always been uniquely centered on one man--Abimaél Guzmán. Guzmán's methods and goals are similar to those of the Khmer Rouge, "including a total rejection of modernity," which he associated with imperialism.[24]

Sendero seemingly cared very little for its own lives and even less for those of any Peruvians or foreigners who sought to help Peru out of its deprivation and abject misery. Its goal was to drive the country into such utter chaos that the people would be compelled to rise up en masse in a revolt against the government. Sendero, though initially hesitant to take on the church because of its popularity, began to attack church leaders in the early 1990s to eliminate any competitors to its influence and to further push Peru into the abyss of anarchy and despair, a necessary step to its ultimate goal. Analysts debate whether Sendero's own particular breed of violence was completely wanton and indiscriminate. In some instances its acts seemed pointless and unprovoked, and in most cases categorically devoid of any moral constraints or limitations.

Leadership

The PCP operated illegally throughout much of its existence. Because of the clandestine nature in which it was forced to operate, loyalties evolved centered on dominant personalities rather than the party as a whole. Out of this environment, and seeking a purer form of communism, Abimaél Guzmán became the central figure and sole leader of the Sendero movement. Guzmán's authority and control within the organization have been described as being a "charismatic leader-follower relationship," which is characterized by a leader, Guzmán, who possesses a unique vision of the future and is credited with almost superhuman qualities, and group followers, who accept the leader's views unquestioningly and obey his orders without hesitation, and with total devotion.[25] Guzmán views himself as a "revolutionary Moses who will lead his followers across a river of blood into the promised land of communism."[26]

Guzmán was born out of wedlock in 1934 in Arequipa. His father was a middle-class merchant who ensured that Guzmán received a complete education, sending him to a Jesuit high school and San Agustin University, where he received degrees in philosophy and law. While studying at the university, two men heavily influenced Guzmán: Kantian philosopher Miguel Rodriguez Rivas and Stalinist painter Carlos de la Riva, who helped radicalize his philosophy from social democrat to Marxist-Leninist.[27] In 1962, Guzmán accepted a professorship at UNSCH, where he "discovered the peasantry and started to understand Chairman Mao." In 1965, Guzmán went to China to attend a cadre school, where his devotion to Maoist principles became ingrained.[28] After his return, numerous splits and rivalries within the PCP led eventually to Guzmán's organization of Sendero, initially only a secretive political organization. In 1976, Guzmán resigned from the university to devote all his efforts to his revolution. With the exception of Julio Cesar Mezzich, who joined in 1980, Guzmán and his original followers remained Sendero's top leadership.[29] The Shining Path, much like supporters of Mao Tse-Tung, followed and revered its leader with a fanatical and almost religious zeal. Sendero insurgents referred to their leader as "Presidente Gonzalo" and firmly believed that he was the "fourth sword of Marxism"--after Marx, Lenin, and Mao and the leader of the new communist world revolution. Prior to his capture, he ran Sendero with rigid megalomaniacal control. Guzmán's enigmatic leadership directly contributed to Sendero's strength. Not markedly striking in appearance, Guzmán was exceptionally persuasive. In the 1980s, Guzmán dominated Sendero but was rarely personally seen by anyone but his closest supporters. Guzmán was cast in an inscrutable, mystical light as a result of Sendero's complex cellular structure and the godlike reverence with which most Senderistas held him.

As alluded to previously, increased emphasis on education and the control of the university education program allowed Guzmán significant influence over a more enlightened and increasingly disgruntled audience, spreading the Maoist Sendero message resulting in "many public universities [becoming] virtual Senderista training grounds."[30] Leadership beneath Presidente Gonzalo was derived predominantly from his own students from UNSCH, who were caught up in Guzmán's fervor and charisma. Sendero's subordinate elements were broken up into cells, much like modern-day transnational terrorist groups, to fight the people's war. Each of these subordinate cells had its own leadership, focused on the common goal; however, Sendero remained firmly under the control of its authoritarian leader. Such rigidity and fixation on one man, according to some, is what led to the collapse of Sendero following Guzmán's capture. Alternatively, this almost deification of Guzmán helped to keep the movement focused on its goal and led to almost no splinter factions and a distinct unity of effort. The subordinate leaders will be discussed in greater detail below, but Sendero clearly remained very centralized in its decision making at the national level under the leadership of Guzmán, nicknamed "Shampoo" in his university days because of his purported ability to brainwash.[31] Nevertheless, Guzmán was captured on 12 September 1992. Following a call for all of his followers to lay down their arms and a renunciation of violence in January 1994, his central role seemed to come to an end. Sendero did not die out completely, and, though it has never been proven, some believe Guzmán still influences what is left of Sendero today from his jail cell on San Lorenzo Island submarine base, offshore from the port of Callao.[32]

Organization

Sendero was organized along a rigid hierarchical and pyramidal structure with five different levels of participation: (1) Guzmán and top leaders (*cupola*), forming the national directorate and central committee, where national decisions were made; (2) commanders (*cuadros*), who managed the regional zones; (3) militants, who executed the campaign of violence; (4) activists, who distributed information, organized demonstrations, and educated the populace; and (5) a national group of sympathizers, who took part in demonstrations, contributed resources, and provided other support.[33]

By the middle of 1992, the height of Sendero's popular war, estimates of guerilla strength in Peru included between 5,000 and 6,000 armed militants and an active support network of about 50,000, with tens of thousands more providing support as a result of intimidation and coercion.[34] Evidence acquired from Sendero's records captured in 1992 reflected over 23,000 armed militants, indicating the government's severe underestimation of Sendero strength.[35] Nonetheless, even at the height of Sendero's power, these figures were a mere fraction of Peru's over twenty-two million people.

While Sendero considered the *campesinos* the significant revolutionary force, they included only a select few in the first three levels of leadership described above.

Having sought early in the 1980s to motivate them to rise up, Sendero found it extremely difficult to fully integrate the masses into its people's war. Because of Sendero's ideological rigidity and unwillingness to allow its ideals to be diluted by expanding its core membership to include parts of the Peruvian legal left, Sendero kept the scope of its insurgent organization somewhat narrow. Any analysis of Sendero leaves no doubt that Sendero's leadership was not from the proletariat. Sendero's recruitment strategy focused on expanding its popular support bases but its vetting process of new recruits and clashes with community leaders in rural areas led to minimal conscription from the lower classes. In fact, the majority of Sendero's recruits came from young middle-class recalcitrant mestizo youth from provincial towns who came to feel that their education would not guarantee them the opportunities in Peruvian society to which they felt they were entitled.[36] Having not achieved the desired levels of popular participation, they modified their tactics and resorted far more frequently to coercion and intimidation to mobilize the people. This tactic met with moderate success when government presence to counterbalance Sendero influence was absent, but overall it kept the scope of the insurgency movement somewhat small and its organization somewhat elitist.

      Sendero's organization was "structured along rigid, close-knit and secretive lines."[37] Such a secretive and clandestine organization made it one of the toughest insurgencies in history to effectively counter. Elements of the Peruvian government aggressively pursued Sendero leaders unsuccessfully for over a decade. Senderologists agree that the party is very authoritarian and bureaucratic when it comes to long-range strategic planning and major political decisions, with power tightly held at the top. In regards to implementing policy and executing the war, it is considerably decentralized.

Sendero's militants were believed to be organized into local cells made up of no more than five to nine members organized and isolated from the other cells for security reasons, making it very difficult for a traitor to inform on a large portion of the group.[38] Analysts go on to point out that, while decentralization did enhance security for the organization, it posed serious communications and command and control problems, leading to excesses by local cadres.[39] To help enhance its communication, Sendero began using its newspaper, *El Diario*, to unify the efforts of its cells and give guidance to its subordinate cadres.[40] Nevertheless, the complexity of the organization has proven both beneficial and detrimental to its success. Its decentralized organization made it largely impermeable to Peruvian counterintelligence operations but also undermined its ability to unify its efforts and implement a strategy that could gain broad-based popular support. Sendero's failure to combat the Peruvian government utilizing all of the instruments of national power will be discussed at greater length below.

Finally, Sendero remained remarkably cohesive and, unlike many Latin American insurgencies, saw virtually no schisms or splinter factions. Unconfirmed reports indicated that rivalries and rifts did exist, including one between the Eastern Regional Committee, which controlled the coca-rich UHV, and the national central committee as they vied for control of the drug money. Suspicion also existed that in the late 1980s Sendero split into an urban-based political terrorist group led by Guzmán and a rural-based guerrilla group under the command of Julio Cesar Mezzich after a disagreement over the best strategy to employ.[41] None of these reports, however, were confirmable in alternate sources and, for the most part, Sendero has always appeared united in its cause. Until Guzmán's capture, Sendero remained decidedly under the headship of one man.

It is also interesting to point out that, although Sendero tenaciously adhered to its belief in revolutionary violence as the one true path, internal debates did take place. Debates within Sendero took the form of a dialectical discussion, called "two-line struggles," in which two sides formed with a hardliner communist "red line" on one side and a more pragmatic opposite. Through this process, self-criticism and analysis occurred, allowing the party to make necessary adjustments to its strategy and tactics. Once the debate was over, however, the party made a collective decision and all were expected, to the point of death, to adhere to it.[42] Tina Rosenberg confirms this zealous expectation of blind acceptance of the party line as she quotes a Senderista, dubbed Javier, as saying: "Men can be wrong, but not the party. The party is never wrong."[43] Also indicative of its cohesion is the method in which recruits transition from activist to militant participant, involving extremely comprehensive background security checks and a demonstrated willingness to obey orders unquestioningly.[44]

Sendero's scope, complexity, and cohesion proved both constructive and deleterious with regard to its ability to prosecute the people's war. On the one hand, when combined with its doctrinaire ideology and decentralized cellular organization, Sendero proved very cohesive and one of the toughest Latin American insurgencies to eradicate. Alternatively, its ideological rigidity and intolerance of passive or other approaches for achieving communist utopia stymied its efforts to expand its popular support. Sendero's rejection of all other communists as opportunists, thus limiting the scope of their organization, unambiguously hampered its efforts and prolonged the struggle.

Insurgent Strategy According to the Instruments of National Power

The following section focuses on the strategy employed by Sendero during its people's war and their use or failure to use the instruments of national power. In order to organize this analysis of Sendero's strategy, five periods are used: 1965 to1980--before the violence and building consensus and infrastructure; 1980 to 1983--the formative years; 1983 to1987--expanding and concentrating on rural violence; 1987 to 1992-- transition to urban strategy and height of power; and 1992 to 2002--the end of potency. During each of these periods, Sendero's overall strategy evolved as it focused to varying degrees on each of the instruments of national power, some more effectively than others.

<u>1965 to 1980: Before the Violence--Building Consensus and Infrastructure</u>

Following Guzmán's return from China, he became convinced of the need for a Chinese-style popular revolution to overcome Peruvian corruption and economic disparity. In the early 1970s, Sendero was scarcely different from the scores of other student-based radical organizations that typified Peruvian educational centers. Between 1970 and 1977, Sendero maintained a low profile. During this time, Sendero formulated its ideology, initial base of support, and theory of victory.[45] Guzmán resigned his post at UNSCH in 1976, going underground to dedicate himself full time to Sendero. The more focused efforts at forming a cohesive and united people's communist party began ostensibly in 1976. During his last years at UNSCH, however, Guzmán broadly spread his revolutionary message in his classroom. Many of his students, in turn, became teachers in schools in the interior and propagated the same message, focusing on the utility of education for escaping historical oppression and discrimination.

Focusing on building popular bases of support, Guzmán sent numerous student cadres to the Amerindian population to provide direct services and benefits that had been consistently neglected by the central government, believing that "propaganda takes place through actions."[46] In this manner, Guzmán created limited parallel hierarchies to win the hearts and minds of the *campesinos*. Approaching the towns pragmatically, Sendero cadres displayed interest in learning about their problems. This approach, however, endured only briefly until the early 1980s. Turning to armed struggle, Sendero provided very little in the way of services to the Amerindians but demanded much in terms of commitment to their ideology. It is unclear why Guzmán turned so dramatically to a military-focused campaign in 1980. In fact, he faced some opposition to it from within in 1979.[47] Perhaps Guzmán recognized that in the 1970s and 1980s "the expansion of participatory democracy in Latin America delegitimized [many] revolutionary movements . . . [and] from El Salvador to Chile, violent revolutionaries lost their raison d'etre as democracy grew and citizens gained real roles in governing their own affairs."[48]

<u>1980 to 1983: The Formative Years</u>

In many cases, insurgencies align themselves with regional or international powers for a host of reasons. The primary reason, typically, is to garner economic support for their cause, including money or military advisers. Diplomatically, reasons for seeking external alliances range from seeking to build legitimacy in the eyes of one's own people, to exert pressure on the regime through a stronger hegemonic power in the international arena, or to gain a voice on the international stage. Sendero explicitly and consistently renounced ties with other countries that might have attempted to dilute or influence the purity of its true communism. Its disdain for modern communism, represented by North

Korea, China, and Cuba, has been discussed above, but its actions speak even louder than words. In the late 1980s, Sendero bombed a North Korean commercial office in Lima and has consistently spoken out strongly against the opportunistic, revisionist regimes in China and Cuba.[49] In his treatise, Developing Guerrilla War, dated 1982, Guzmán vilified Deng Xiao-Ping as a "traitor to the international communist movement."[50]

Denouncing diplomatic efforts, Sendero also refused to engage in any negotiations with the Peruvian government, citing gross corruption and claiming that armed struggle was the only vehicle for change in Peru. Efforts were made by both the Belaúnde government in 1982 and the García government in 1985 and 1986 to bring Sendero to the negotiating table, all of which were rebuffed.[51] This position did not change until after Guzmán was captured. Consistent with its efforts in the late seventies, Sendero continued to assertively preach its message in the rural towns of Ayacucho in order to win popular support and participation by the peasantry in the people's revolution. In the early 1980s, Sendero propagandists entered towns periodically, demanding widespread attendance at and participation in Sendero ideology classes and indoctrination sessions. In order to secure popular support, Sendero would often transfer money, livestock and other goods for distribution amongst the community, which won limited favor among some peasants and alienated others.[52] Such dogmatic rhetoric and refusal to cooperate with other communists decidedly hurt Sendero's chances for success by removing valuable allies for their cause. Ironically, Sendero's ideological communist purity, Guzmán's justification for these denunciations, was clearly tainted by his exploitation of the capitalistic drug-trade which funded his campaign.

Beyond just proselytizing, however, Sendero portrayed itself as the defender of indigenous culture, vociferously denouncing the efforts of the police and Drug Enforcement Agency to eradicate coca cultivation and replace it with less profitable crop substitution.[53] For coca growers, this stance became a selling point for Sendero, as Sendero's involvement in the drug trade began to help fix prices between the coca growers and the drug traffickers. In expanding its role in the drug trade, Sendero made inroads into a lucrative and endless source of wealth for its underequipped guerrillas.

Sendero's military campaign began on the eve of 17 May 1980 with the destruction of ballot boxes in Ayacucho villages; however, Sendero was, at that time, severely underfunded and ill equipped.[54] Its military strategy in the first couple of years was characterized by low-tech and small-scale attacks, and was, by its own admission, "modest, almost without modern weapons."[55] The largest attack during this period involved an attack on a prison in Ayacucho City by fifty to sixty armed militants to free fifty-four Senderistas.[56] Statistics indicate that the number of terrorist attacks attributed to Sendero climbed markedly from 193 in 1982 to 695 in 1984 to 1,327 in 1986, demonstrating Sendero's increasing focus on violence and coercion.[57]

Sendero eschewed foreign alliances and external support out of disdain for all other communist regimes, including the Soviet Union. Guzmán believed that true communism died out with Stalin. Unable to rely upon foreign aid for its funding, Sendero began to expand its control into the key coca-producing regions and solidified its position as the arbitrator between the coca farmers and the Colombian cocaine manufacturers. Sendero established its base of operations in the early 1980s in the Upper Huallaga Valley, which provided in excess of 30,000 hectares of coca leaf production for the drug trade. In addition, by 1984, Sendero began to establish control over a number of the dirt airstrip runways used by the drug traffickers to ship the coca leaves to labs in Colombia. Seizing opportunities to expand its resource base, Sendero began to tax drug traffickers between $5,000 and $15,000 per flight at an estimated 120 Sendero-controlled airstrips.[58]

During the earlier part of the 1980s, Sendero did attempt to supplant the government by providing services, including primarily education, limited relief, and aid, but only in Ayacucho. Becoming increasingly more focused on its military component, Sendero efforts to subvert the government by winning popular support through economic aid and parallel hierarchies dwindled.

1983 to 1987: Expanding and Concentrating on Rural Violence

Though initially committed to winning the information campaign and the popular support of the *campesinos*, Sendero has never been willing to collaborate with the legal most popular political parties that the peasants supported. The majority of the lower class in the early 1980s threw its support behind the American Popular Revolutionary Alliance (APRA) and the United Left (*Izquierda Unida*-IU). Sendero consistently attacked IU groups, dubbing them "parliamentary cretins" who stood as obstacles to the success of the people's revolution.[59] This stance not only endured but also intensified as Sendero increasingly viewed the legal left as one of the primary impediments of the revolution.

Although, Sendero generally steered clear of political participation, it did seek to infiltrate the political establishments to further its cause. By the late 1980s, evidence indicated that Sendero had infiltrated a number of legal organizations. A Senatorial aide, a respected Catholic seminarian, elected community and union leaders, military and police recruits, and even some would-be nuns were among such Sendero infiltrators.[60]

Such efforts did not indicate that Sendero wanted to utilize legal nonviolent means to gain power, but instead merely reflected the extent to which Sendero was willing to go to extend its intelligence apparatus to provide greater protection for its military campaign. Infiltration of these organizations was geared towards providing early warning for governmental and military efforts to combat Sendero and to help subvert legal efforts to compete against Sendero in the interior.

Growing more focused on its military campaign and frustrated at the apathy of the peasantry, Sendero curtailed its provision for the rural communities except for propaganda through indoctrination and the schools that had long been infiltrated by cadres of Sendero teachers. With a decline in the services and assistance provided by Sendero relative to the early 1980s, many peasants found Sendero's ideology less appealing and began to resist. The combined escalation of Sendero bloodshed and the pressure to ascribe to Sendero ideology with little-to-no offer of tangible provision alienated the peasants, and Sendero soon found itself facing even more resistance and apathy from the *campesinos*. By the 1986, it appeared far less committed to winning converts to its cause based on ideology. Additionally, due to its ideological fixation, Sendero, to subvert the capitalist system, began shutting down peasant markets, further alienating many and leading to an escalating cycle of repression.[61] By the late 1980s, Sendero's information campaign diminished to convincing peasants that Sendero would brutally eliminate any competitors and that cooperation with government, aid and relief organizations, or foreign commercial interests in Sendero-held territory would lead to severe reprisals. Efforts to indoctrinate the *campesinos* with their ideology diminished to near insignificance, as Sendero's strategy became militarily focused.

In the mid-1980s, 15-to-20-percent of Peru's population lived in "pink" or "red" zones under a significant or predominant Sendero influence. The majority of these citizens provided their support for Sendero; however, they did so out of intimidation or fear not ideological affinity.[62] By the mid 1980s, it became clear that Sendero's focus was less on garnering broad-based popular support than on neutralizing the populace as a player. Ostensibly, Sendero realized that it was struggling to mobilize the *campesinos* and recognized that if the people were not with them, they could easily be against them.

Fighting the stronger and better-resourced government forces, Sendero chose to transition its efforts vis-à-vis the masses to ensuring that they stayed out of the struggle. Its method of accomplishing this by the mid-1980s, and in response to the Belaúnde and García governments' expanding military presence in Sendero-held regions, was to ruthlessly intimidate and threaten the people in the towns so that the *campesinos* chose not to assist the government or any other relief agencies. In the mid-1980s, when Sendero entered a new area, it immediately set out on a campaign of threats against the local authorities, conducted selective assassinations, denied the rights of other institutions of any kind to exist, and began to coerce all in the area to submit to its demands upon fear of torture, rape, or murder.[63] The point of this violence was to so terrorize the population that they would refuse to assist the government in any way and allow Sendero to focus its efforts on government agencies and legitimacy. This strategy also sought to deepen the suffering of the Peruvian people to precipitate a total rebellion of the proletariat.

By the mid 1980s, Sendero secured its funding by expanding its alliance with the drug traffickers. By 1987, it appeared to have a firm control on the hired guns, the *sicarios* of the Colombian traffickers, who until Sendero entered the drug business had brutally abused and cheated coca growers.[64] Sendero also expanded this control to the other coca-producing areas, including in the departments of Ayacucho, Huancavelica, Apurímac, Junín, Huánuco, and portions of Ancash and Cusco, earning between twenty and fifty million dollars annually for its cause.[65] Documents captured in 1989 proved that Sendero's involvement in narcotics trafficking added significantly to its war reserves and military strength with, for example, thousands of Belgian-made assault rifles bought from the drug traffickers, enhancing Sendero's ability to compete with the counterinsurgency forces militarily. This money also helped fund salaries for militants, ranging between 250 and 1,000 dollars per month, and support families of fallen heroes.[66]

<u>1987 to 1992: Transition to Urban Strategy and Height of Power</u>

In the mid- and late-1980s, military and police counterinsurgency campaigns became increasingly repressive and human rights violations abounded. Sendero reaped some small benefits from this backlash, as governmental excesses, such as the 1986 prison massacre of some 270 Senderistas, began to drive more students and some members of the radical left into the hands of Sendero.[67] Some of these new adherents, who were used to political organizing as former members of the IU, decided to try to champion Sendero's cause in public forums, thus gaining more publicity for Sendero's goals. Sendero's leadership remained opposed to taking formal steps to integrate into the legal political process, remaining committed to communism achieved through violence. Nevertheless, the publicity for Sendero's political aims did benefit Sendero indirectly. Though reaping some benefits from these new politically active sympathizers, Sendero remained formally opposed to any cooperation with the "reactionary politicians of the IU" and charged that all existing popular organizations, such as legal political parties, unions, and even competitor insurgency MRTA, were obstacles to the success of the people's revolution. Demonstrating this sustained animosity for the legal left, Sendero guerillas exploded dynamite at an IU rally in Lima, wounding four workers and Jorge del Prado, the leader of the PCP.[68] Much like Sendero's refusal to ally with international communists, such animosity toward the legal left, though assisting in keeping their organization under the tight control of one leader, undermined any efforts to expand their cause and perpetuated the perception that Sendero was a fanatical extremist group.

By the mid 1980s, Sendero appeared to give up on winning popular support and became increasingly more focused on its military campaign to ensure that the populace remained nonaligned. This strategy did not change in the late 1980s, as Sendero continued to target key leaders and international relief agencies that stymied Sendero's efforts. In the early and mid 1980s, Sendero did not dare attack the church institutions or clergy because of the very positive public image that the church enjoyed in Peru. However, by the early 1990s, and based in no small part on the strength that Sendero enjoyed at this stage, almost reaching the point of strategic equilibrium, Sendero decided that everyone was fair game. Between September 1990 and June 1992, Sendero assassinated "five pastoral agents, two nuns, and three priests" to eliminate any competitors.[69] As would be expected, this did not endear Sendero to much of the population, who relied on the church relief organizations in no small way for aid.

On the other hand, evidence provided in other sources indicates a strategic shift in the late-1980s with regard to Sendero's propaganda. Whereas in the mid-1980s it reduced its indoctrination crusade in the interior in favor of a singularly military campaign, following its first plenary session in September 1987 Sendero's leaders endorsed a strategic shift with regards to its efforts at publicizing its goals. Following this meeting, it held public meetings at San Marcos University, distributed pamphlets, posters, and banners, sent revolutionary messages to the media, and even agreed to the first ever media interview with Guzmán in January 1988.[70] Additionally, Sendero began to co-opt the media by securing *El Diário*, a Lima-based daily with a distribution of 5,000.[71] The government closed it in late 1988 after the editor was accused of being a member of Sendero, but it reappeared in 1989 as a weekly and continued to spread Sendero rhetoric, albeit more diluted. Nevertheless, popular support at this stage remained poor, in spite of Sendero's renewed efforts. This was evidenced by the paltry attendance of a mere 250 activists in May 1988 at a Sendero rally in Lima.[72] Compared to the 30,000 who marched through the streets of Lima on 12 November 1989 chanting, "Say yes to democracy," it is clear that Sendero was losing the information war.[73] In fact, by early 1991, few Peruvians viewed Sendero as anything more than terrorists and 68-percent believed that Sendero presented the number one threat to the country as a whole.[74]

Sendero expanded its campaign of violence so much that its own records documented 63,052 armed actions between 1987 and 1989 and 23,090 in 1990 alone, compared to the 6,692 between 1980 and 1983 and 28,621 between 1983 and 1986.[75] Exploiting a growing rift between police forces and military in the provinces under emergency control, in April 1989 Sendero conducted a massive attack on an Uchiza police garrison, slaughtering many, but they underestimated the revulsion their actions would cause among the masses.[76] Following this armed action, thousands were easily persuaded to enthusiastically accept Peruvian military control.

Sendero also expanded its circle of victims, as it began to target more public officials. Sendero assassinated APRA leaders such as Deputy Secretary of the APRA Nelson Pozo and Economic Minister Rodrigo Franco between 1987 and 1990.[77] Additionally, Sendero assassinated thirteen IU politicians between 1987 and 1992.[78] In a campaign of destabilizing violence leading up to the 1989 elections, Sendero assassinated more than eighty mayors, leading to the resignation, out of fear, of around 400 other candidates.[79] One of its most renowned assassinations occurred in February of 1992. The brutal murder of María Elena Moyano, described previously, backfired and served to galvanize public outrage against Sendero-inflicted carnage.[80]

Sendero's urban campaign was characterized by daily destruction, including random car bombs, widespread power outages, and supermarket bombings, and resulted in about 83-percent casualties among unarmed civilians. Despite inroads in the cities, capitalizing on the abject poverty in the *pueblos jóvenes*, this cycle of wanton violence eroded Sendero's limited support, yet increased the perception that Sendero might actually succeed in toppling the government.

By the early 1990s, Peru had become the world's leading producer of coca leaves. The marriage of Sendero and the drug traffickers was profitable to all involved. By the 1990s, some estimates place Sendero's profit from this alliance at up to one hundred million dollars annually.[81] Secure in its funding, Sendero focused narrowly on its military campaign. In terms of providing for the people's economic malaise, Sendero efforts waned. With the decision to merely neutralize versus mobilize the masses, Sendero appealed only to the most belligerent segments of society and lost any hope of winning proponents by portraying itself as a viable alternative to the regime.

1992 to 2002: End of Potency

The near-mystical aura surrounding Guzman quickly dissipated after his capture in 1992, as he was portrayed as a broken and frail middle-aged man who frequently got drunk, not the superhuman that most Senderistas believed.[82] After catching Guzmán, his close aide "Comrade Miriam," and virtually Sendero's entire political bureau, Sendero violence waned. For the next sixteen months, Senderistas, dealt a severe blow with the incarceration of their leader, lashed out hoping to regain lost ground. Though still deadly, their violence at this point seemed to lack the direction and organization it had had with Guzmán at the helm. Then in February 1994 Guzmán ordered those of his supporters still at large to engage in a peace process with the government. There is little explanation for such a radical shift except theories that he was exhausted with the war and perhaps felt helpless to run it from prison; his call for peace was made with hopes of receiving amnesty, political status, and better prison conditions.[83] At this point, Sendero effectively split into two factions: those who advocated Guzmán's peace process and those who sought to continue the armed struggle. Thousands of former Senderistas laid down their arms and accepted offers of amnesty from the Fujimori government.[84]

Leading the breakaway faction, called *Sendero Rojo*, and outraged at the concessions Guzmán called for, "Comrade Feliciano," Alberto Durand, extolled the need to continue the revolution.[85] Under "Feliciano," violence continued, but far less frequently. In a bid to win some of the support Sendero held under Guzmán, Durand "rounded up locals for political talks, admitting past errors and claiming to have renounced terrorism."[86] Having lost much its momentum, though, Feliciano was incapable of amassing the same support for the revolution as Guzmán had. The *Rojo* rebels spent the majority of their time running from counterinsurgency forces in the jungles and effectively disappeared after Durand's capture on 14 July 1999.[87] As of the completion of this thesis, a small segment (estimated at a few hundred) of Sendero remained in the interior under the leadership of "Comrade Artemio," Cerdón Cardoza. Sendero's campaign of violence, ideological indoctrination, and control of the drug trade is a faint specter of its former strength. The only Sendero attack of any significance in recent years was a car bombing at a Lima supermarket near the US embassy in March 2002. Though some claim that Sendero could be regaining strength, a return to the nightmarish violence of the early 1990s is improbable.

Guzmán's Sendero long parted ways from the Maoist principles that he claimed to follow in three significant ways: (1) in contrast with Sendero's rigid authoritarian control and seizure of all local authority, Mao called for peasant groups to "have more or less complete control;" (2) unlike Sendero's fixation with carnage, Mao warned against "the strategic dangers associated with the abuse of violence, especially in relation to the necessity of cultivating consent from the masses;" and (3) despite Mao's admonition that a revolution "can neither exist nor flourish if it separates itself from [the masses'] sympathies and cooperation," Sendero clearly abandoned real efforts to garner popular support.[88] The sources of Sendero's failures are evident in these departures from Mao's principles and the government's eventual success in finding Sendero's Achilles heel.

Analyzing Governmental Response and Strategy

Despite Sendero's failures, the Peruvian government appeared at times inept and ill prepared to deal with Sendero--explaining one of the reasons why Sendero endured. As David Scott Palmer testified before the House Foreign Affairs Committee, "revolutions do not succeed; governments fail."[89] Sendero, which sprang from humble beginnings, grew to such potency in the late 1980s and early 1990s not only because of what it did but also because of what the government failed to do. Governments that maintain a monopoly on the legitimate use of force must be cautious about using that force indiscriminately. The military instrument of national power is often the primary and occasionally the sole instrument of national power used by the government in its counterinsurgency efforts. As Peru in the 1980s demonstrated, chronic underestimating of insurgent capabilities and influence, excesses in the use of the military and police, and failure to attack the roots and goals of the insurgency will inevitably lead to an enduring revolution that could have been crushed much earlier if countered properly.

Governmental Response

Any nation-state faced by an intractable revolutionary movement like Sendero must devise a response that eliminates the military threat while simultaneously reducing the potential for resurgence by coping with the root causes of the insurgency. As the Peruvian experience demonstrates, in some cases, it is essential to attack these categories simultaneously to enhance the chances for successful counterinsurgency. In suspending the Peruvian Constitution, shutting down Congress and the courts, imprisoning political opponents, and announcing rule by decree, President Fujimori vowed he could finally target Sendero and promised to eliminate the threat by 1995. He essentially succeeded, but how and why? What did Fujimori do that had been missing from the efforts of his predecessors? Many of the state's failures have already been detailed; however, for the sake of synopsis, the following addresses Peruvian counterinsurgency strategies employed under the three different presidential administrations between 1980 and 2000.

The Belaúnde Administration (1980 to 1985)

The virulent campaign of terror and subversion unleashed by Sendero caught the Belaúnde government completely by surprise. Despite Sendero's substantial presence in Ayacucho by 1982, Belaúnde refused to take the group seriously, dismissing them as mere criminals and thugs.[90] When the government finally realized that Sendero was a substantial security threat, its reaction was too little, too late, and ultimately counter-productive. The government sent special counterinsurgency forces, the *Sinchis*, to Ayacucho, giving them a free hand. As Sendero turned increasingly to brutal violence to neutralize the *campesinos*, the military concocted its policy of indiscriminate terror to intimidate the rebels into submission, leaving the *campesinos* caught between the two. Counterinsurgency techniques, often applied indiscriminately, resulted in severe human rights violations against the civilian population and created more recruits for Sendero. By the end of Belaúnde's term in 1985, over 6,000 Peruvians had died from the violence, and over one billion dollars in property damage resulted.[91] Not all Peruvian leaders agreed with this strategy, as General Adrián Huamán, a Peruvian departmental commander in the early 1980s, urged leaders to promote developmental assistance. Ignored, he was removed from office in 1984.[92] Human rights violations soared between 1984 and 1986. Strongly criticized by international human rights organizations, Belaúnde nevertheless continued to rely on military solutions rather than other social or developmental measures that could address the fundamental underlying socioeconomic causes of the insurgency.

After the cultivation of coca for narcotics uses was made illegal in 1978, efforts to curtail production were intensified by the Belaúnde government, under pressure from the US These measures alienated the growers and enhanced the spread of Sendero into the

UHV in 1983-1984 as defenders of the growers. Sendero flourished at a time when it was most vulnerable because Belaúnde ignored the roots of insurgency, myopically focused on a misguided oppressive military strategy, and ignored the need for popular support.

The García Administration (1985 to 1990)

Alan García came to power in 1985 and made some inroads in the war against Sendero in the early years by curtailing the military's brutality, insisting that it show respect for human rights. He directed considerable developmental assistance, largely through zero-percent-interest agrarian loans and institution of public works projects in the interior, leading to 100,000 jobs.[93] Unfortunately for García, development initiatives were hindered by the abysmal national economy by 1987, spawned by his shortsighted decision to cut repayment of national debt to 10-percent of exports. As the economy began to plummet and García's efforts to improve the socioeconomic conditions faltered, Sendero continued to gain power and shifted its focus into the urban areas. In 1989, General Alberto Arciniega, assigned to the Huallaga emergency zone following the Uchiza massacre, launched an aggressive counterinsurgency attack while allowing the coca growers to continue their trade unimpeded and initiating goodwill-building civic actions, such as well digging and providing electricity.[94] In spite of the failing economy, military efforts like this began to regain the faith of the people in the government.

Though late in his presidency, García continued to punish human rights violations within the military, began implementing reforms in the intelligence system, and proposed expanded use of the *ronda campesinos*, self-defense units comprised of peasants heavily armed by the government so that they could defend themselves against Sendero.[95] These measures demonstrated his understanding of the need to win broad-based support, exercise judicious but skilled military strategies, and address economic roots of the discontent; but his mismanagement of the economy and alienation of the international community resulted in drastic cuts in foreign aid and investment, severely undercutting any efforts to use the diplomatic and economic instruments of national power. Also, severe pay cuts for the military and zealous efforts to indict human rights violators in the armed forces strained his relationship with his primary tool to counter a potent Sendero.

<u>The Fujimori Administration (1990 to 2000)</u>

Peru had long been working with other nations to help recover from its economic collapse. Austerity programs made conditions progressively worse in the 1980s. Additionally, by 1990, US attention remained narrowly focused on counterdrug efforts, since American politicians were more concerned with solving problems directly affecting the US Carrying baggage from the American experience in Central America, the US Congress sought to separate counterdrug and relief funds from the counterinsurgency funds, making the latter inaccessible until human rights records improved. According to most analysts, this missed the point, which Fujimori clearly understood. The problem of cocaine production was inextricably linked with the insurgency crisis because of the marriage between Sendero and narcotics trafficking. Fujimori, recognizing the need for foreign aid, also knew that it had to be on terms that would contribute to Sendero's defeat across a multidimensional front. In September 1990, Fujimori turned down 35.9 million dollars in US aid because of US fixation with counterdrug strategies to the exclusion of all else.[96] This strategy eventually paid off as the US, desperate to take concrete action in the drug war, began to provide both counterdrug and economic assistance.

In 1990 Peru had one of the freest presses in the world, with virtually no checks on what was published. The state-owned channel provided fairly well balanced news. Peru's media were varied, competitive, and highly informative. Though free, the media clearly favored the government and very little positive press was given to Sendero. Adept at using the media to its advantage, the government, aired on national television a video of Guzmán dancing in a drunken stupor in 1991.[97] Additionally, following Guzmán's arrest, Fujimori "opportunistically framed the capture in a sensational media spectacle, culminating with a picture of Guzmán [in prison stripes] in a circus-style animal cage."[98]

As alluded to above, the interservice contempt between police and military came to a head in 1989 when Sendero attacked the Uchiza police station. Despite desperate pleas by the police chief for military assistance, just minutes away by helicopter, no military relief arrived and the Uchiza post fell by morning, with every policeman murdered.[99] Expanding initial efforts by García, Fujimori worked hard to fix this problem by enhancing cooperation between the police and military, revitalizing and integrating intelligence activities, and extensively using the *ronda campesinos*. Under Fujimori, the *rondas* reached an estimated 232,668 *ronderos* to help protect the citizens against Sendero, who even at its strongest fielded only 10-percent of that. The *rondas* worked well because sponsorship of these groups by the government placed autonomy and responsibility for the local security back in the hands of the local authorities.[100]

Detailed above, the removal of the obstacles to reform in the 1992 *autogolpe* (self-coup) significantly enhanced Fujimori's ability to implement reforms unfettered by the bureaucracy. Though hugely unpopular internationally, his actions met with an 80-percent approval at home as Peruvians were invigorated by the thought of a leader prepared to do what it takes to end the carnage.[101] Furthermore, Fujimori reinstituted democracy a mere seven months later with elections for the Democratic Constituent Congress on 22 November 1992, reestablishing the conditions necessary for the return of foreign aid.[102] Unfortunately, rights violations did occur under Fujimori, including about 2000 "disappearances" from 1990 to 1996. There was also speculation that a quarter of the "terrorists" imprisoned were innocent, but these excesses occurred as they were beating Sendero and were tolerated in the euphoria of victory over this twelve-year long blight.[103] Some experts, like David Palmer, saw the *autogolpe* as a setback for both democracy and the war against Sendero; however, the record indicates that, due to the rampant corruption within the system, victory was far less likely without it. Although it is dangerous to automatically start justifying the ends with the means, it is clear to this author that the *autogolpe* was a necessary step to defeat corruption and Sendero.[104]

Fujimori challenged the military to reform so that it could defeat the insurgency by being the "vanguard of the struggle for development and social justice."[105] Following this challenge, the Army improved its small-unit tactics, revitalized its intelligence system, curtailed its excesses, and improved its image by instituting civic action programs. The Fujimori government launched an ambitious 300-million-dollar road repair program, which by 1992 included repairs to 1,400 kilometers of the Pan American and Central Highways and maintenance of 2,000 kilometers of the other roads.[106]

Fujimori, though hugely unpopular at first due to his "Fujishock" measures aimed at regaining control of the economy, became overwhelmingly popular by 1992, as most Peruvians finally saw a leader who appeared competent and visionary. His economic measures also helped to revitalize the economy, bring back foreign investment and aid, and slash inflation dramatically. Recognizing the importance of attacking the roots of discontent in the interior and source of income to Sendero, Fujimori also provided aid to motivate UHV *campesinos* to stop coca cultivation and try something new. He provided 2,100 agricultural loans, 4,700 land titles, and 1,256 kilometers of roads; he rehabilitated twelve bridges, reducing travel time by 60-percent, and built thirty-eight potable water systems, sixteen medical posts, and eighty-eight water pumps.[107]

In summary, Fujimori's success resulted from his ability to utilize all of the instruments of national power to counter Sendero's goals. Diplomatically, he reversed a disastrous economic policy that stymied efforts to garner international assistance to beat Sendero and he successfully maneuvered the US into supporting multidimensional solutions to the interconnected drug, insurgency, and underdevelopment problems. He capitalized on the informational instrument through well-publicized revitalization programs and mobilization of the masses through the *rondas* and other measures aimed at garnering popular support. Militarily, he targeted Sendero where it was weakest through improved intelligence to capture Guzman and his central leadership; reformed the poor public image of the Peruvian military and police; and removed the stumbling blocks of rampant congressional and judicial corruption, which had hampered his reforms and the counterinsurgency's effectiveness. Economically, he successfully regained control of the failing economy by reopening Peruvian markets and enticing foreign aid again.

---

[1]Michael Radu, "Can Fujimori Save Peru?" *Bulletin of the Atomic Scientists* 48, no. 6 (July/August 1992): 19.

[2]Ian E. W. Beckett, *Modern Insurgencies and Counter-Insurgencies: Guerrillas and Their Opponents Since 1750* (New York, NY: Routledge, 2001), 84.

³James F. Rochlin, *Vanguard Revolutionaries in Latin America* (Boulder, CO: Lynne Rienner Publishers, 2003), 32.

⁴Sandra Woy-Hazleton and William A. Hazleton, "Sendero Luminoso: A Communist Party Crosses a River of Blood," 62-83, in *Political Parties and Terrorist Groups*, ed. Leonard Weinberg (London, England: Frank Cass and Company, Ltd., 1992): 65.

⁵Miguel Esperanza, "Terrorism in Peru," *America* 166, no. 21 (20 June 1992): 538.

⁶Woy-Hazleton and Hazleton, "Sendero Luminoso: A Communist Party," 62.

⁷Linda H. Flanagan and William Rosenau, "Blood of the Condor: The Genocidal Talons of Peru's Shining Path," *Policy Review* 59 (winter 1992): 82.

⁸Bernard W. Aronson, "Peru's Brutal Insurgency: Sendero Luminoso," *US Department of State Dispatch* 3, no. 12 (23 March 1992): 237-238.

⁹Ibid., 238.

¹⁰Anthony Daniels, "No Light, No Law," *National Review* 42, no. 21 (5 November 1990): 33.

¹¹Flanagan, and Rosenau, 83.

¹²Aronson, 237.

¹³Rochlin, 71.

¹⁴Beckett, 84.

¹⁵Bard E. O'Neill, *Insurgency and Terrorism: Inside Modern Revolutionary Warfare* (McLean, VA: Brassey's Publishing, 1990), 17.

¹⁶Eliab S. Erulkar, "The Shining Path Paradox," *Harvard International Review* 12, no. 2 (winter 1990): 43.

¹⁷Woy-Hazleton and Hazleton, "Sendero Luminoso: A Communist Party," 63.

¹⁸Sandra Woy-Hazleton and William A. Hazleton, "Sendero Luminoso and the Future of Peruvian Democracy," *Third World Quarterly* 12, no. 2 (April 1990): 23.

¹⁹Henry Dietz, "Revolutionary Organization in the Countryside: Peru," 117-139, in *Revolution and Political Change in the Third World*, ed. Barry M. Schutz and Robert O. Slater (Boulder, CO: Lynne Rienner Publishers, 1990), 124.

[20] Patrick W. Symmes, "Out to Lunch with Sendero," *American Spectator* 24, no. 12 (December 1991): 28.

[21] Aronson, 236.

[22] Woy-Hazleton and Hazleton, "Sendero Luminoso: A Communist Party," 69.

[23] Ibid.

[24] Radu, 17.

[25] Gordon H. McCormick, *The Shining Path and the Future of Peru* (Santa Monica, CA: RAND Press, 1990), 7.

[26] Orin Starn, "New Literature on Peru's Sendero Luminoso," *Latin American Research Review* 36, no. 2(2001): 219.

[27] Woy-Hazleton and Hazleton, "Sendero Luminoso: A Communist Party," 65-66.

[28] Ibid.

[29] Ibid.

[30] Radu, 19.

[31] Cynthia McClintock, *Revolutionary Movements in Latin America: El Salvador's FMLN and Peru's Shining Path* (Washington, D.C.: United States Institute Peace Press, 1998), 262.

[32] Rochlin, 71.

[33] Dietz, 128.

[34] David Scott Palmer, "Peru, the Drug Business and Shining Path: Between Scylla and Charybdis," *Journal of Interamerican Studies and World Affairs* 34, no. 3 (fall 1992): 69.

[35] Rochlin, 63.

[36] Woy-Hazleton and Hazleton, "Sendero Luminoso: A Communist Party," 73.

[37] Dietz, 128.

[38] Woy-Hazleton and Hazleton, "Sendero Luminoso: A Communist Party," 71.

[39] Ibid.

⁴⁰McCormick, *The Shining Path*, 8.

⁴¹Woy-Hazleton and Hazleton, "Sendero Luminoso: A Communist Party," 72.

⁴²Ibid., 70.

⁴³Tina Rosenberg, "Guerrilla Tourism," *New Republic* 202, no. 25 (18 June 1990): 24.

⁴⁴Dietz, 128.

⁴⁵McCormick, *The Shining Path*, 4.

⁴⁶Woy-Hazleton and Hazleton, "Sendero Luminoso: A Communist Party," 67.

⁴⁷Ibid., 70.

⁴⁸Aronson, 238.

⁴⁹Ibid., 237.

⁵⁰Woy-Hazleton and Hazleton, "Sendero Luminoso: A Communist Party," 70.

⁵¹McCormick, *The Shining Path*, 13.

⁵²McClintock, *Revolutionary Movements in Latin America*, 292.

⁵³Woy-Hazleton and Hazleton, "Sendero Luminoso and the Future of Peruvian Democracy," 24.

⁵⁴McCormick, *The Shining Path*, 15.

⁵⁵Rochlin, 60.

⁵⁶McCormick, *The Shining Path*, 17.

⁵⁷Ibid., 25.

⁵⁸Palmer, "Peru, the Drug Business and Shining Path," 67.

⁵⁹Woy-Hazleton and Hazleton, "Sendero Luminoso: A Communist Party," 70.

⁶⁰Radu, 18.

⁶¹McClintock, *Revolutionary Movements in Latin America*, 293.

⁶²Aronson, 237.

[63] Esperanza, 539.

[64] McCormick, *The Shining Path*, 22.

[65] Radu, 18.

[66] McClintock, *Revolutionary Movements in Latin America*, 292.

[67] Woy-Hazleton and Hazleton, "Sendero Luminoso and the Future of Peruvian Democracy," 23.

[68] Ibid.

[69] Esperanza, 539.

[70] Woy-Hazleton and Hazleton, "Sendero Luminoso and the Future of Peruvian Democracy," 23.

[71] Rex A. Hudson, *Peru: A Country Study* (Washington, D.C.: Library of Congress Press, 1993), 240.

[72] Woy-Hazleton and Hazleton, "Sendero Luminoso and the Future of Peruvian Democracy," 23.

[73] Erulkar, 45.

[74] Hudson, 125.

[75] Rochlin, 61-64.

[76] William Rosenau, "Poor Peru," *American Spectator* 23, no. 12 (December 1990): 17.

[77] McCormick, *The Shining Path*, 20.

[78] Woy-Hazleton and Hazleton, "Sendero Luminoso and the Future of Peruvian Democracy," 23.

[79] McClintock, *Revolutionary Movements in Latin America*, 294.

[80] Rochlin, 64.

[81] Palmer, Peru, the Drug Business and Shining Path, 67.

[82] McClintock, *Revolutionary Movements in Latin America*, 263.

[83] Carlos R. Izaguirre, "Shining Path in the 21st Century," *NACLA Report on the Americas* 30, no. 1 (Jul/Aug 1996): 37.

[84] Rochlin, 71-72.

[85] Ibid.

[86] "Flickers from the Past: How Big a Threat is the Shining Path?" *Economist* 368, no. 8333 (19 July 2003): 28.

[87] Ibid.

[88] Rochlin, 75-76.

[89] Aronson, 238.

[90] Hudson, 241.

[91] Ibid., 54.

[92] Rochlin, 65.

[93] Ibid., 66.

[94] Rosenau, 17.

[95] Rochlin, 69.

[96] Palmer, "Peru, the Drug Business and Shining Path," 68.

[97] Hudson, 240.

[98] Rochlin, 71.

[99] Palmer, "Peru, the Drug Business and Shining Path," 68.

[100] Rochlin, 69.

[101] Ibid., 67.

[102] Hudson, 208.

[103] Rochlin, 70.

[104] Palmer, "Peru, the Drug Business and Shining Path," 71.

[105] Flanagan and Rosenau, 84.

[106] Hudson, 163.

[107] Aronson, 239.

CHAPTER 6

CONCLUSIONS

Conclusions to Be Drawn About the Peruvian Case Study

Woy-Hazleton and Hazleton claim that Sendero's endurance resulted from: (1) Sendero's ability to modify its agenda and structure to absorb new followers; (2) its territorial and institutional expansion where the government was weakest, enhancing their relative strength; and (3) its continual escalation of violence to undermine the rules of the democratic regime, forcing the government to resort to reprisals that were adverse to its own legitimacy.[1] This assessment only partially explains Sendero's staying power.

Diplomatic Instruments of National Power

Clearly, Sendero's strengths were often its greatest weaknesses. Its ideological rigidity contributed positively by preserving the cohesiveness of the organization, but it also prevented both integration of popular support and leaders of the legal left and assistance from international and regional powers. The treatment of Guzmán with deity-like veneration led most followers to respond to Guzmán's directives with perfunctory, unqualified obedience and yet proved to be the Achilles heel of its organization when Guzmán was captured and exposed as a mere mortal. Despite adhering to the same theories of protracted popular war and revolutionary violence, Comrades "Feliciano" and "Artemio" have been unsuccessful at mobilizing much more than a few hundred supporters. Essentially with Guzmán's mystique dispelled, governmental efforts to attack Sendero and the roots of Peruvian discontent resulted in Sendero's downfall.

Based on Sendero's fixation with the war within the Peruvian borders, one would think that it would be unnecessary for the government to capitalize on the diplomatic instrument of national power. Indeed, in the case of other insurgencies, where insurgents aggressively pursue diplomatic overtures to gain sympathy and aid for their struggle, diplomatic efforts to counter these efforts are especially important. However, as Sendero not only has chosen not to pursue alliances and aid from outside sources but has also categorically renounced all ideologically similar governments as cretins, one might believe that the Peruvian government could afford to ignore this instrument of national power. On the contrary, however, the Peruvian government began to make its most significant gains and successes in its war against Sendero when it recognized its need to gain the support of the international community. García, late in his presidency, and Fujimori both sought to implement strategies to overcome the impediments to garnering US and international support by reforming the military, curbing human rights violations, and insisting on certain key elements of support to facilitate its war on both narcotics and insurgency, which were inextricably interwoven. In doing so, Fujimori succeeded at shaping US support to match his needs and the needs of his country by forcing US support to address not just the counterdrug goals that the US Congress desired but also aid for the Peruvian military and economic aid. In doing so, Fujimori demonstrated that, despite the lack of any need to directly counter any diplomatic measures by the insurgents, the use of the diplomatic instrument of national power could still prove useful and essential to his strategy as it helped shore up weaknesses in his military and economic instruments of national power.

Informational Instruments of National Power

Sendero endorsed Mao's protracted popular war and initially appeared to work diligently at building broad-based popular support. One of the key steps to gaining this is to actively engage in an information campaign that capitalizes on the propaganda machine, works to educate the people on the nature and righteousness of their cause, and seeks to gain a voice in and support from the media. Initially, Sendero appeared to be committed to such a campaign. However, as it began to focus on revolutionary violence, became obsessed with disbanding capitalist peasant markets, and sought to jealously protect its influence in the insurgent-held areas by destroying aid structures, Sendero rapidly lost the popular support it needed. Seeing its information campaign failing, Sendero then dismissed its losses in popular support as apathy and weakness from indigenous masses and determined that it could decide what was best for the people, and settled for neutralization rather than support of the peasants. This strategy, in fact, largely sealed Sendero's fate and severely limited Sendero's chances for ultimate victory, albeit successfully extending the hurricane of violence for many more years.

The Fujimori government readily recognized the importance of a successful information campaign and implemented an aggressive effort to discredit Sendero, using the media to portray Sendero and Guzman specifically as misguided, inept, and habitually drunk. As governmental efforts to discredit Sendero gained momentum, the Fujimori government took it a step further and mobilized the masses against Sendero through the *rondas*. In this manner, by convincing the people that Sendero was a poor choice for their allegiance and by expanding opportunities and authority for autonomy and local control throughout the interior under the tempered guidance of the central government, Fujimori again effectively countered Sendero's attempts to keep the *campesinos* neutral and mitigated his weaknesses in the military instrument of national power.

Chapter 3 outlined a number of conditions that foment insurgencies; one of the gravest challenges that can perpetuate rebellion in spite of comprehensive and competent counterinsurgency efforts is to need to rectify discrimination based on ethnic or religious lines that fosters deep-rooted prejudices and rigid class systems. In Peru, rifts are unmistakable along centuries-old ethnic lines where to this day, an age of purported enlightenment and equal opportunity in open democratic societies, Amerindians are victimized solely because of age-old narrow-mindedness. Though governments may take limited steps to correct such discrimination as part of their information campaign, it is often mere lip-service. In countries where such conditions exist, it is essential that the government take concrete steps to correct the prejudices in the culture inasmuch as it is possible. So long as governments treat certain segments of society as second-class citizens and exclude them from the real and tangible benefits of pluralistic society, the conditions for insurgency will remain. Even if the government is successful at defeating a particular insurgent group, the conditions will continue to breed more.

Military Instruments of National Power

Sendero's pathological dependence on escalating and brutal violence as the means to successful revolution neutralized much of the population and plunged the country deeper into the despair that was Sendero's espoused goal. While Sendero's overreliance on the military instrument to the detriment of all others may have resulted in preserving and extending the life of the insurgency, it progressively moved the chances for revolutionary success farther and farther from its grasp as the consensus grew that Sendero was more of a malevolent blight on Peru than a viable political alternative to the existing regime. The government, on the other hand, implemented a strategy synthesizing the instruments of national power to directly counter both the goals and the roots of the insurgency. By increasing the professionalism, competence, restraint, and intelligence skill of the military, Fujimori was able to better target and locate Sendero's vulnerability, its leadership, and then work its way down through the rest of its organization as it floundered following the blow of losing its authoritarian leadership.

Economic Instruments of National Power

Finally, Sendero's move to control the drug trade in Peru provided it with tremendous economic self-sufficiency, providing better weaponry and relatively good salaries for its soldiers. However, this double-edged sword weakened its ideological credibility, as narcotics trafficking represented unrestrained capitalistic opportunism, the very institution that Sendero claimed to oppose. Inability or refusal to create parallel hierarchies and implement the economic instrument of national power, particularly in the early 1990s and especially in light of these tremendous financial reserves, demonstrates how Sendero lost its way from the true path of Mao. As Peru faced economic collapse under García and struggled to recover under Fujimori, Sendero could have achieved significant gains by making greater overtures to alleviate the poverty of the masses and by seeking greater broad-based popular support. As it is, Sendero achieved a maximum estimated number of around 23,000 militants, a mere one-tenth of a percent of Peru's population, demonstrating its limited popularity.

The Peruvian governments that struggled to eliminate Sendero's influence did so, initially, on an extremely narrow and one-dimensional path of military counterinsurgency strategy. In doing so, they failed to understand the importance of attacking the root causes of the insurgency in the first place. Failing to implement broad-based economic policy designed to undermine the sources of discontent only extended the life of the insurgency. Late in his presidency, García realized this and began efforts to tackle his country's pervasive economic problems, but was faced with ineffectual economic policy and half-measures that was doomed to fail. Fujimori, fully understanding the critical import of his country's economic situation, aggressively pursued economic reforms and demanded that the United States contribute to both economic aid and counterdrug programs to successfully tackle his problems. It was only through these efforts in the late 1980s and the early 1990s, fully appreciating the economic instruments of national power, that the Peruvian government began to gain the upper hand and the economic initiatives helped to ensure that, when combined with Sendero's ruthlessness, the Peruvian people would see hope in the government and nothing but evil in the insurgency.

Sendero's close-knit and cellular organization, which confounded government efforts to penetrate it; the unlimited funding generated by Sendero's control of Peru's narcotics trafficking; and its willingness to escalate the level of violence without regard for any moral codes, especially in the face of the misguided and myopic strategy of governmental counterinsurgency, explains why this particular insurgency endured for so long. Sendero's refusal to utilize all of the instruments of national power, its inability to garner the broad-based popular support called for under true Maoist insurgency theory, and its obsession with one man, when combined with a counterinsurgency strategy that finally attacked the insurgents across the entire spectrum, ultimately led to its demise.

General Conclusions

There is much utility in analyzing both the insurgency's and the government's use of the instruments of national power, particularly in concert with its assessment of its adversary's goals, strengths, and weaknesses. One must recognize that there is limited cross-applicability for generalizations in terms of the specific strategies applied by the government and insurgents in the Peru to other insurgencies due to significant differences between the cultural, ethnic, and religious patterns of people and the strategies and goals employed by the insurgents in Peru when compared to others. The Peruvian case study, nonetheless, does demonstrate the importance of employing all of the instruments of national power in an insurgent or counterinsurgent strategy and the importance of targeting an adversary's goals. By analyzing the steps taken by the government to combat insurgency, one can see how efforts that appear to be broad and aggressive can actually miss the most effective means to defeat an insurgency. Governments that fail to target an insurgent group's goals, strengths, and weaknesses using all the instruments of national power are destined to extend the life of that insurgency. Similarly, insurgents who fail to attack the government where it is weakest and to implement all of the instruments of national power can also expedite their own demise. The instruments of national power however are not a panacea for the elimination of all insurgencies, but, through the analysis of these instruments, there is some limited predictive value, within a margin of error, to explain why insurgencies endure in the face of significant opposition. By reorganizing O'Neill's steps and adding the analysis of insurgent and governmental use of the instruments of national power, this thesis has sought to propose a better framework for analyzing enduring insurgencies and to answer the primary thesis question.

Suggestions for Future Research

At the outset of this project, the goal was to conduct a two- or three-case-study analysis using the methodology outlined in chapter 3. Because of the depth of the methodology and the wealth of information available in the Peruvian case study, this rapidly exceeded the limitations of this thesis. The methodology is nonetheless sound and would benefit from further testing against other case studies to corroborate the emphasis that this thesis places on applying all instruments of national power.

Insurgency warfare has grown even more important and relevant in light of current events, and given the recognition that both joint and Army doctrine and military journalism have given to the US military's role in combating insurgencies, and the terrorism employed by many insurgents, it is essential to fully understand the magnitude and relevance of utilizing all of the instruments of national power. The US military is increasingly called upon to implement national policy abroad, beyond just conventional military tools, in order to succeed in the current War on Terror and to bring stability to the unstable regions. In doing so, US Army professionals must remember that to win in a counterinsurgency one must first drain the swamp and then go after the alligators--the proper application of all of the instruments of national power are essential to this task.

---

[1]Sandra Woy-Hazleton and William A. Hazleton, "Sendero Luminoso and the Future of Peruvian Democracy," *Third World Quarterly* 12, no. 2 (April 1990): 22.

GLOSSARY

For a better understanding of the body of work in this thesis, it is necessary to outline and explicitly delineate a number of key terms and their connotations, as they are applied throughout this research project.

Autogolpe: A coup organized by the government itself to allow it to take extra powers.[1]

Campesinos: A native of a Latin-American rural area; especially: a Latin-American Indian farmer or farm laborer.[2]

Conventional Warfare: Joint Publication 1-02, *Department of Defense Dictionary of Military and Associated Terms*, does not provide a definition for this term. As it is one of the three key forms of warfare adopted by insurgents, a definition is important to providing a proper background for this thesis. According to Bard O'Neill in his seminal work on insurgency, conventional warfare is "the direct confrontation of large units in the field."[3]

Counterinsurgency: Counterinsurgency is a complex idea, addressing the diverse methods and frameworks for combating insurgency. Coming to a common definition for all governments is difficult at best because of the complexities and disparities in insurgency motives, strategies and characteristics from region to region and state to state. Joint Publication 1-02 provides the following definition: "those military, paramilitary, political, economic, psychological, and civic actions taken by the government to defeat insurgency."[4] In his book entitled, *Modern Insurgencies and Counter-Insurgencies*, Ian Beckett defines counterinsurgency as "those military, political, socio-economic and psychological activities employed by the authorities and their armed forces to defeat the threat in question."[5] Both definitions address the psychological operations that are instrumental to winning the hearts and minds and in regaining the popular support that is so frequently lost by the government to successful insurgents, but they do not address the informational tools that must be employed. As such, the definition used for this study is a synthesis of these definitions to include those military, paramilitary, political, economic, social, psychological, and informational actions undertaken by the government to counter and defeat insurgencies.

Creole: a person of European descent born especially in the West Indies or Spanish America; a person of mixed French or Spanish and black descent, speaking a dialect of French or Spanish.[6]

Democracy: Insurgencies arise in a wide variety of environments and governments, ranging from democracies, communist governments, authoritarian dictatorships, and many others. Because one of the most common remedies for insurgency is purportedly democracy, it is necessary to explicitly define this term. Neither Joint Publication 1-02 nor Field Manual 1-02 define democracy; therefore, for the purposes of this study, Terry Karl's definition of "democracy" or "democratic government" will be used: "a set of institutions that permits the entire adult population to act as citizens by choosing their leading decision-makers in competitive, fair, and regularly scheduled elections which are held in the context of the rule of law, guarantees for political freedom, and limited military prerogatives."[7] Not all governments that claim to practice democracy ascribe to this definition. It is, after all, somewhat narrow. For the purpose of this thesis, however, it is important to specify what constitutes a legitimately democratic government, as at different points in the history of Latin America, some authoritarians claimed to provide liberal democracy to their people, but in reality restricted the just expression of beliefs of many of their citizens by denying them suffrage. Additionally, this definition is important because it provides adequate emphasis on the need to subordinate the military to the rule of civilian leadership – a tenet that has long been a core foundation of American democracy, without which at any time that the military does not approve of the policies of the national leadership, military authorities are believed likely to usurp power.

Desborde popular: overflowing of the masses, which was typical of the mass migration from the interior to the coastal regions in Peru in the late 1980s.[8]

Docenio: the twelve-year rule of the military regime in Peru from 1968 to 1980.

Guerrilla Warfare: Joint doctrine stipulates that guerilla warfare is the "military and paramilitary operations conducted in enemy-held or hostile territory by irregular, predominantly indigenous forces."[9] Che Guevara, in his book entitled *Guerilla Warfare* defines it as "the case of an armed group engaged in a struggle against the constituted power, whether colonial or not, which established itself as the only base and which builds itself up in rural areas."[10] Bard O'Neill describes guerilla warfare as one of the three forms of warfare associated with insurgent conflicts, joining the other two, which are terrorism and conventional warfare. According to O'Neill, guerilla warfare is characterized by "highly mobile hit-and-run attacks by lightly armed groups that seek to harass the enemy and gradually erode his will and capability."[11] Guerilla warfare is also characterized by a realization that, because of relative advantages in strength of the adversary, attacks will be indirect and will be aimed at focusing the guerillas' strengths against the government's weaknesses or vulnerabilities in short engagements. The synthesis of these definitions and characteristics leads to a better understanding of this essential tool of insurgency.

Insurgency: Defining "insurgency" specifically is critical to understanding this phenomenon. According to JP 1-02, insurgency is "an organized movement aimed at the overthrow of a constituted government through the use of subversion and armed conflict."[12] Although this is a sufficient definition for the field manuals, it omits several critical points. For the purposes of this study, the definition of insurgencies found in the Central Intelligence Agency pamphlet, *Guide to the Analysis of Insurgency*, is constructive:

> Insurgency is a protracted political-military activity directed toward completely or partially controlling the resources of a country through the use of irregular military forces and illegal political organizations. Insurgent activity — including guerrilla warfare, terrorism, and political mobilization — is designed to weaken government control and legitimacy while increasing insurgent control and legitimacy. The common denominator of most insurgent groups is their desire to control a particular area. This objective differentiates insurgent groups from purely terrorist organizations, whose objectives do not include the creation of an alternative government capable of controlling a given area or country.[13]

This definition helps clarify some of the ambiguities left in the joint definition. There are several distinctions drawn in using this definition. Insurgent organizations differ from purely terrorist organizations in that civil violence is perpetrated within national boundaries to accomplish political mobilization, destabilize the existing government, exercise control over specific regions within national boundaries, and develop greater political legitimacy for the insurgent movement. In insurgencies, violence is typically a means to an end to create a new government, force concessions from an existing government, or preserve certain policies in a political construct that may imminently change. Terrorism is still frequently an integral strategy of insurgencies, but in the context of this study, terrorism represents specific tactics that are used as part of a broader strategy to destabilize a government or to force societal or political change. O'Neill's definition of insurgency complements an understanding of this phenomenon. He defines insurgency as "a struggle between a non-ruling group and the ruling authorities in which the non-ruling group consciously uses political resources (e.g., organizational expertise, propaganda, and demonstrations) and violence to destroy, reformulate, or sustain the basis of legitimacy of one or more aspects of politics."[14]

Insurgent: According to JP 1-02, an insurgent is a "member of a political party who rebels against established leadership."[15] This definition is almost accurate, but fails to recognize that in some cases insurgents have no direct links to specific political parties and may be focused on military strategy as a precursor to political activity. Mao Tse-Tung insisted in his theory of protracted popular war that for an insurgency to succeed it must pay equal attention to both the political and military dimensions. In Che Guevara's writings, however, focused on military-focused strategy, lesser importance is acceded to the political dimension. Under these circumstances, it is important to expand the definition provided in the joint doctrine to include members of other organizations who rebel against established leadership, and not just members of a political party. Latin American revolutionary history is replete with examples of upheavals initiated by the military and not political parties.

Insurgent Group: It follows that an "insurgent group or organization" is any organization that actively participates in or advocates activities designed to weaken government control and legitimacy while increasing its own control and legitimacy.

Mestizo: person of mixed blood; specifically: a person of mixed European and American Indian ancestry.[16]

Narco-terrorism: Narcotics play an integral and inseparable role in many Latin American insurgencies, especially so in the case study selected for this study--Sendero. Initially serving as a means to an end to fund their insurgency activities, recent trends have shown that the integration of narcotics trafficking and insurgency has led to a rise in narco-terrorism. Joint doctrine defines narco-terrorism as "terrorism conducted to further the aims of drug traffickers. It may include assassinations, extortion, hijackings, bombings, and kidnappings directed against judges, prosecutors, elected officials, or law enforcement agents, and general disruption of a legitimate government to divert attention from drug operations."[17]

Pueblos jóvenes: the underdeveloped shantytowns surrounding Lima and the other metropolises in Peru.[18]

Relative Deprivation: An integral part of the theories on what causes insurgencies is the theory of relative deprivation. For the purposes of this thesis, the definition found in Ted Gurr's book, *Why Men Rebel*, will be used. Relative deprivation is defined as a perceived discrepancy between the goods and conditions of life to which people believe they are entitled as a matter of right, and the realization of the goods and conditions that they are capable of acquiring, given the means available to them.[19]

Revolutionary: According to joint doctrine, "an individual attempting to effect a social or political change through the use of extreme measures."[20]

Subversion: According to joint doctrine, subversion is any "action designed to undermine the military, economic, psychological, or political strength or morale of a regime."[21]

Terrorism: As discussed above, terrorism is a means to an end for insurgents. Joint doctrine defines terrorism as "the calculated use of unlawful violence or threat of unlawful violence to inculcate fear; intended to coerce or to intimidate governments or societies in the pursuit of goals that are generally political, religious, or ideological."[22] Bard O'Neill describes terrorism as one of the three forms of warfare associated with insurgent conflicts, joining the other two, which are guerilla warfare and conventional warfare. His definition provides a better and more focused explanation of terrorism as it relates to insurgency and is more relevant for this research study. Terrorism is a form of warfare "in which violence is directed primarily at noncombatants, rather than operational military or police forces or economic assets." Insurgent terrorism is focused, rather than gratuitous, violence because terrorists seek to change the political community, political

Terrorist: Joint doctrine, when taken in conjunction with O'Neill's definition of terrorism, adequately defines a terrorist as an individual who uses violence, terror, and intimidation to achieve a result.[24]

Unconventional Warfare: Unconventional warfare is "a broad spectrum of military and paramilitary operations, normally of long duration, predominantly conducted by indigenous or surrogate forces who are organized, trained, equipped, supported, and directed in varying degrees by an external source. It includes guerrilla warfare and other direct offensive, low visibility, covert, or clandestine operations, as well as the indirect activities of subversion, sabotage, intelligence activities, and evasion and escape."[25]

---

[1] The Oxford Spanish Dictionary (1994), s.v. "Autogolpe."

[2] Webster's Third New International Dictionary (1981), s.v. "Campesino."

[3] Bard E. O'Neill, *Insurgency and Terrorism: Inside Modern Revolutionary Warfare* (McLean, VA: Brassey's Publishing, 1990), 26.

[4] Department of Defense, Director for Operational Plans and Joint Force Development (J-7), JP 1-02, *The Department of Defense Dictionary of Military and Associated Terms* (Washington, DC: US Government Printing Office, 12 April 2001 as amended 17 December 2003), 127.

[5] Ian E. W. Beckett, *Modern Insurgencies and Counter-Insurgencies: Guerrillas and Their Opponents Since 1750* (New York, NY: Routledge, 2001), viii.

[6] Webster's Third New International Dictionary (1981), s.v. "Creole."

[7] Terry Karl, *The Vicious Cycle of Inequality in Latin America* (Madrid: Centro de Estudios Avanzados en Ciencias Sociales, 2002), 2.

[8] Rex A. Hudson, *Peru: A Country Study* (Washington, D.C.: Library of Congress Press, 1993), 4.

[9] Department of Defense, JP 1-02, *The Department of Defense Dictionary of Military and Associated Terms*, 227.

[10] Ernesto "Che" Guevara, "Guerilla Warfare," 37-181, in *Guerilla Warfare: Case Histories of Guerilla Movements and Political Change*, ed. Brian Loveman and Thomas M. Davies (Lincoln, NB: University of Nebraska Press, 1985), 51.

[11]O'Neill, 25.

[12]Department of Defense, JP 1-02, *The Department of Defense Dictionary of Military and Associated Terms*, 260.

[13]Central Intelligence Agency, *Guide to the Analysis of Insurgency* (Washington, D.C.: Central Intelligence Agency, 1986), 2.

[14]O'Neill, 13.

[15]Department of Defense, JP 1-02, *The Department of Defense Dictionary of Military and Associated Terms*, 260.

[16]Webster's Third New International Dictionary (1981), s.v. "Mestizo."

[17]Department of Defense, JP 1-02, *The Department of Defense Dictionary of Military and Associated Terms*, 355.

[18]Hudson, 95.

[19]Ted Robert Gurr, *Why Men Rebel* (Princeton, NJ: Princeton University Press, 1970), 13.

[20]Department of Defense, JP 1-02, *The Department of Defense Dictionary of Military and Associated Terms*, 458.

[21]Ibid., 509.

[22]Ibid., 531.

[23]O'Neill, 24-25.

[24]Department of Defense, JP 1-02, *The Department of Defense Dictionary of Military and Associated Terms*, 531.

[25]Ibid., 550.

APPENDIX A

FIGURES

Phase I: Setting the Stage

Step 1: Provide historical context including general relevant facts on the formation of the country

Step 2: Define the Environment:
1. Physical:
   - Terrain: Safe Havens/Geography
   - Climate
   - Transportation-Communications Infrastructure
2. Human:
   a. Demographic Distribution
   b. Social Structure:
      - Historical proclivity for violence
      - Class system and ethnic discrimination
      - Levels of education
      - Levels of crime
   c. Economic Factors:
      - Disparity between the Haves and the Have-nots
      - Relative Deprivation
      - Unemployment
      - Poor Health Conditions
   d. Political Culture and System

Phase II: Analyzing the Insurgents

Step 3: Provide a brief history of the insurgent group involved in the case study.

Step 4: Classify the type of insurgency according to Bard O'Neill's seven types of insurgency:
1. Anarchist   5. Secessionist
2. Egalitarian   6. Reformist
3. Traditionalist   7. Preservationist
4. Pluralist

Step 5: Define the insurgent strategy employed according to the primary broad categories:
1. Conspiratorial
2. Protracted popular-war
3. Military Focus
4. Urban

Step 6: Define the insurgent organization
1. Ideology
2. Goals
3. Leadership
4. Organization

Step 7: Describe the insurgent tactics and strategy in specific terms IAW their access to the instruments of national power:
1. Diplomatic
   - Efforts to garner support internally from other political groups or externally for their cause
2. Informational
   - Ability to articulate cause to the people....to the world – efforts to gain popular support
   - Insurgent vs. governmental access and use of the media
3. Military
   - Access to weapons suitable to countering governmental high-tech advantage
   - Use of violence as means to coerce change or gain popular support
4. Economic
   - Efforts to bribe or extort populace to support insurgents
   - Efforts to supplant government – parallel hierarchies
   - Influence of drugs and criminal activities in supporting insurgency

Phase III: Analyzing the Governmental Response

Step 8: Describe the governmental response to counter insurgencies:
1. Diplomatic
2. Informational
3. Military
4. Economic

Conclusions and Recommendations for Future Research

Figure 1. Author's Modified Methodology for this Case Study

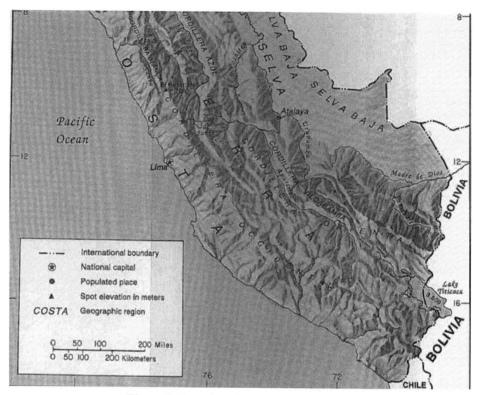

Figure 2. Peruvian Geographical Regions

Source: Rex A. Hudson, *Peru: A Country Study* (Washington, D.C.: Library of Congress Press, 1993), 66.

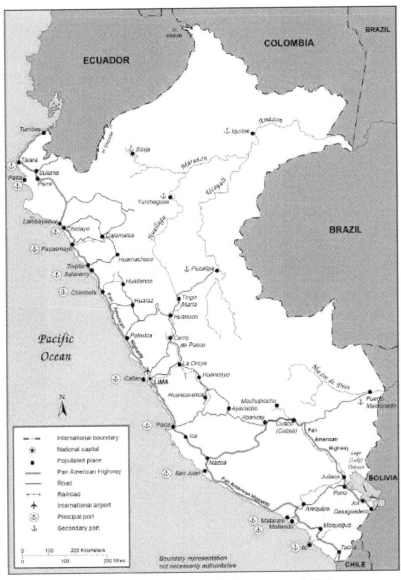

Figure 3. Peruvian Transportation Infrastructure (1991).

Note: Demonstrates the limited road and rail networks supporting movement from the interior to the coastal areas.

Source: Rex A. Hudson, *Peru: A Country Study* (Washington, D.C.: Library of Congress Press, 1993), 162.

Figure 4. Peruvian Geographical Map Reflecting Departments

Source: University of Texas Library, Perry-Castañeda Library Map Collection, 10 February 2004; [database on-line] available from http://www.lib.utexas.edu/maps/peru.html; Internet; accessed on 15 February 2004.

APPENDIX B

TABLES

Table 1. Population and Percentage Growth of Major Cities, Census Years 1961-90

City	\multicolumn{4}{c	}{(in thousands)}	Total Percentage Growth
	1961	1972	1981	1990	
Lima and Callao	1,641	3,394	4,836	6,414	290
Arequipa	158	304	447	634	301
Trujillo	103	241	355	531	415
Chiclayo	95	189	280	426	348
Cusco	79	120	182	275	248
Piura	72	126	186	324	350
Huancayo	64	115	165	207	152
Chimbote	59	159	216	296	401
Iquitos	57	111	185	269	359
Ica	49	73	111	152	210
Sullana	34	60	80	113	229
Tacna	27	55	92	150	473
Talara	27	29	57	89	229
Pucallpa	26	57	92	129	396
Puno	24	41	66	90	275
Huánuco	24	41	53	86	258
Ayacucho	23	34	68	101	339
Cajamarca	22	37	60	92	318
Huacho	22	36	42	87	278
Pisco	22	41	53	77	250
Pasco	21	47	72	76	211
Juliaca	20	38	77	121	505

Note: Demonstrates the rapid urban population growth from 1961 and 1990.

Source: Rex A. Hudson, *Peru: A Country Study* (Washington, D.C.: Library of Congress Press, 1993), 323.

Table 2. Distribution of Population by Region, Census Years 1940-90

(in percentages)				
Year	Coast	Highlands	Selva	Total
1940	25	62	13	100
1961	39	52	9	100
1972	45	44	11	100
1981	51	41	8	100
1990*	53	36	11	100

*Estimated.

Note: Demonstrates the migration trends from the interior to the urban coastal regions between 1940 and 1990.

Source: Rex A. Hudson, *Peru: A Country Study* (Washington, D.C.: Library of Congress Press, 1993), 324.

Table 3. Distribution of Income by Quintile, 1972 and 1985

(in percentages)		
Quintile	1972	1985
Highest	61.0	51.9
Second	21.0	21.5
Third	11.0	13.7
Fourth	5.1	8.5
Lowest	1.9	4.4
TOTAL	100.0	100.0

Note: Demonstrates the stratification of wealth in Peru.

Source: Rex A. Hudson, *Peru: A Country Study* (Washington, D.C.: Library of Congress Press, 1993), 330.

Table 4. Health Indicators, 1975-90

Heath Indicator	1975	1980-85	1985-90
Public health expenditure per capita[*]	n.a.	n.a.	17.90
Average calories per capita	2,263	2,144	2,277
Food supply as percentage of FAO recommendation[**]	100	99	93
Access to potable water[***]	47	52	52
Life expectancy at birth	55.5	58.6	62.2
Birth rate[4]	40.5	36.7	34.3
Mortality rate[****]	12.8	10.7	9.2

[*] In United States dollars.
[**] FAO--Food and Agriculture Organization.
[***] In percentages.
[****] Per 1,000 population.

Note: Demonstrates the poor health conditions in Peru.

Source: Rex A. Hudson, *Peru: A Country Study* (Washington, D.C.: Library of Congress Press, 1993), 327.

BIBLIOGRAPHY

Books

Almond, Gabriel A., and Sidney Verba. *The Civic Culture*. Princeton, NJ: Princeton University Press, 1965.

Beckett, Ian E. W. *Modern Insurgencies and Counter-Insurgencies: Guerrillas and Their Opponents Since 1750*. New York, NY: Routledge, 2001.

Brinton, Crane. *The Anatomy of Revolution*. New York, NY: Vantage Publishers, 1965.

Byman, Daniel L., Peter Chalk, Bruce Hoffman, William Rosenau, and David Brannan. *Trends in Outside Support for Insurgent Movements*. Santa Monica, CA: RAND Press, 2001.

Correa, Marcial Rubio. "The Perception of the Subversive Threat in Peru." 107-122. In *The Military and Democracy: The Future of Civil-Military Relations in Latin America*. Edited by Louis W. Goodman, Johanna S.R. Mendelson, and Juan Rial.. Lexington, MA: Lexington Books, 1990.

Dietz, Henry. "Revolutionary Organization in the Countryside: Peru." 117-139. In *Revolution and Political Change in the Third World*. Edited by Barry M. Schutz, and Robert O. Slater. Boulder, CO: Lynne Rienner Publishers, 1990.

Gootenberg, Paul. *Between Silver and Guano: Commercial Policy and the State in Post-independence Peru*. Princeton, NJ: Princeton University Press, 1991.

Guevara, Ernesto "Che". "Guerilla Warfare." 37-181. In *Guerilla Warfare: Case Histories of Guerilla Movements and Political Change*. Edited by Brian Loveman, and Thomas M. Davies. Lincoln, NB: University of Nebraska Press, 1985.

Gurr, Ted Robert. *Why Men Rebel*. Princeton, NJ: Princeton University Press, 1970.

Karl, Terry. *The Vicious Cycle of Inequality in Latin America*. Madrid: Centro de Estudios Avanzados en Ciencias Sociales, 2002.

Loveman, Brian, and Thomas M. Davies. *Guerilla Warfare: Case Histories of Guerilla Movements and Political Change*. Lincoln, NB: University of Nebraska Press, 1985.

McClintock, Cynthia. *Revolutionary Movements in Latin America: El Salvador's FMLN and Peru's Shining Path*. Washington, D.C.: United States Institute Peace Press, 1998.

McCormick, Gordon H. *The Shining Path and the Future of Peru.* Santa Monica, CA: RAND Press, 1990.

_____. *From Sierra to the Cities: The Urban Campaign of the Shining Path.* Santa Monica, CA: RAND Press, 1992.

Munck, Ronaldo, and Purnaka L. de Silva. *Postmodern Insurgencies: Political Violence, Identity Formation, and Peacemaking in Comparative Perspective*. New York, NY: St. Martin's Press, 2000.

O'Neill, Bard E. *Insurgency and Terrorism: Inside Modern Revolutionary Warfare.* McLean, VA: Brassey's Publishing, 1990.

Palmer, David Scott. "Peru: Democratic Interlude, Authoritarian Heritage, Uncertain Future." 258-282. In *Latin American Politics and Development.* 3d ed. Edited by Howard J. Wiarda, and Harvey F. Kline. Boulder, CO: Westview Press, Inc., 1990.

Rochlin, James F. *Vanguard Revolutionaries in Latin America.* Boulder, CO: Lynne Rienner Publishers, 2003.

Sanger, Richard H. *Insurgent Era.* Washington, D.C.: Potomac Books, Inc. Publishers, 1967.

Santayana, George. *The Life of Reason.* New York, NY: Charles Scribner's Sons, 1905.

Schutz, Barry M., and Robert O. Slater. *Revolution and Political Change in the Third World.* Boulder, CO: Lynne Rienner Publishers, 1990.

Scott, Andrew M. *Insurgency.* Chapel Hill, NC: University of North Carolina Press, 1970.

Snow, Donald. *Distant Thunder: Patterns in Conflict in the Developing World.* Armonk, NY: M. E. Sharpe, 1997.

Tse-Tung, Mao. *On Guerilla Warfare.* Introduction and translation by Samuel B. Griffin II. Baltimore, MD: The Nautical and Aviation Publishing Company, 1992.

Turabian, Kate L. *A Manual for Writers.* 6th ed. Chicago: University of Chicago Press, 1996.

Walton, John. *Reluctant Rebels: Comparative Studies of Revolution and Underdevelopment.* New York, NY: Columbia University Press, 1984.

Werlich, David P. *Peru: A Short History.* Carbondale and Edwardsville, IL: Southern Illinois University Press, 1978.

Wickham-Crowley, Timothy P. *Exploring Revolution: Essays on Latin American Revolutionary Theory*. Armonk, NY: M. E. Sharpe, 1991.

_____. *Guerillas and Revolution in Latin America: A Comparative Study of Insurgents and Regimes Since 1956*. Princeton, NJ: Princeton University Press, 1991.

Woy-Hazleton, Sandra, and William A. Hazleton. "Sendero Luminoso: A Communist Party Crosses a River of Blood." 62-83. In *Political Parties and Terrorist Groups*. Edited by Leonard Weinberg. London, England: Frank Cass and Company, Ltd., 1992.

Periodicals

Aronson, Bernard W. Peru's "Brutal Insurgency: Sendero Luminoso." *US Department of State Dispatch* 3, no. 12 (23 March 1992): 236-240.

Daniels, Anthony. "No Light, No Law." *National Review* 42, no. 21 (5 November 1990): 30-32.

Erulkar, Eliab S. "The Shining Path Paradox." *Harvard International Review* 12, no. 2 (winter 1990): 43-44.

Esperanza, Miguel. "Terrorism in Peru." *America* 166, no. 21 (20 June 1992): 537-540.

Flanagan, Linda H. and William Rosenau. "Blood of the Condor: The Genocidal Talons of Peru's Shining Path." *Policy Review* 59 (winter 1992): 82-85.

"Flickers from the Past: How Big a Threat is the Shining Path?" *Economist* 368, no. 8333 (19 July 2003): 28-29.

Goodwin, Jeff, and Theda Skopcol. "Explaining Revolutions in the Contemporary Third World." *Politics and Society* 17, no. 4 (December 1989): 489-509.

Holmes, Jennifer S. "Terrorism, Drugs and Violence in Latin America." *Latin American Research Review* 37, no. 3 (2002): 217-230.

Izaguirre, Carlos R. "Shining Path in the 21st Century." *NACLA Report on the Americas* 30, no. 1 (July-August 1996): 37-38.

Kopel, Dave, and Mike Krause. "Losing the War on Terrorism in Peru." *National Review* 22, no. 1 (March 2002), 143-144.

Olney, Patricia, and Michael Radu. "Sendero Luminoso and the Threat of Narcoterrorism." *Orbis* 35, no. 3 (summer 1991): 480.

Neier, Aryeh. "Watching Rights." *Nation* 254, no. 19 (18 May 1992): 657.

Palmer, David Scott. "Peru, the Drug Business and Shining Path: Between Scylla and Charybdis." *Journal of Interamerican Studies and World Affairs* 34, no. 3 (fall 1992): 65-88.

Radu, Michael. "Can Fujimori Save Peru?" *Bulletin of the Atomic Scientists* 48, no. 6 (July-August 1992): 16-21.

Rosenau, William. "Poor Peru." *American Spectator* 23, no. 12 (December 1990): 16-18.

Rosenberg, Tina. "Guerrilla Tourism." *New Republic* 202, no. 25 (18 June 1990): 23-25.

Schulz, Donald E. "The Growing Threat to Democracy in Latin America." *Parameters* (spring 2001): 59-71.

Starn, Orin. "New Literature on Peru's Sendero Luminoso." *Latin American Research Review* 36, no. 2 (2001): 212-226.

Symmes, Patrick W. "Out to Lunch with Sendero." *American Spectator* 24, no. 12 (December 1991): 26-28.

Torrens, James S. "Eyes Open in Peru." *America* 172, no. 9 (13 March 1995): 3-4.

Woy-Hazleton, Sandra, and William A. Hazleton. "Sendero Luminoso and the Future of Peruvian Democracy." *Third World Quarterly* 12, no. 2 (April 1990): 21-35.

<u>Government Sources</u>

Central Intelligence Agency. *Guide to the Analysis of Insurgency*. Washington, D.C.: Central Intelligence Agency, 1986.

_____. *State Failure Task Force Report*. Washington, D.C.: Central Intelligence Agency, 1995.

_____. World Fact Book Country Studies: Peru. 18 December 2003. Database on-line. Available from http://www.cia.gov/cia/publications/factbook/geos/pe.html. Internet. Accessed on 11 January 2004.

Department of Defense. Director for Operational Plans and Joint Force Development (J-7), Joint Staff. Joint Publication 1, *Joint Warfare of the Armed Forces of the United States*. Washington, DC: US Government Printing Office, 14 December 2000.

_____. Director for Operational Plans and Joint Force Development (J-7), Joint Staff. Joint Publication 1-02, *The Department of Defense Dictionary of Military and Associated Terms*. Washington, DC: US Government Printing Office, 12 April 2001 as amended 17 December 2003.

_____. Director for Operational Plans and Interoperability (J-7), Joint Staff. Joint Publication 3-07.4, *Joint Counterdrug Operations*. Washington, DC: US Government Printing Office, 14 February 1998.

Department of State Publication. Country Background Notes: Peru. 4 March 2002. Database on-line. Available from http://state.gov/g/drl/rls/hrrpt/2001/wha. Internet. Accessed on 12 October 2003.

_____. Country Reports on Human Rights Practices – 2001. 4 March 2002. Database on-line. Available from http://www.state.gov/g/drl/rls/hrrpt. Internet. Accessed on 16 November 2003.

Hudson, Rex A. *Peru: A Country Study*. Washington, D.C.: Library of Congress Press, 1993.

Metz, Steven. *The Future of Insurgency*. Carlisle Barracks, PA: Strategic Studies Institute, US Army War College, 1993.

US Army. Command and General Staff College. ST 20-10, *Master of Military Art and Science (MMAS) Research and Thesis*. Ft. Leavenworth, KS: USA CGSC, July 2003.

US Army. Headquarters, Department of the Army, Field Manual 3-07, *Stability Operations and Support Operations*. Washington, DC: US Government Printing Office, February 2003.

Other Sources

Davis, Ted, and Robert Walz. "Power and Theories of International Relations." In *C200: Strategic Studies Readings Book*, C212RA-177-186. Ft. Leavenworth, KS: USA CGSC, July 2003.

Freedom in the World Country Ratings. 2 December 2003. Database on-line. Available from http://freedomhouse.org/ratings/index.htm. Internet. Accessed on 22 January 2004.

Smith, Michael L. *GCI-275 - Peruvian Graffitti*. 7 December 2003. Database on-line. Available from http://www.gci275.com/peru. Internet. Accessed on 18 January 2004.

University of Texas Library. Perry-Castañeda Library Map Collection. 10 February 2004. Database on-line. Available from http://www.lib.utexas.edu/maps/peru.html. Internet. Accessed on 15 February 2004.

INITIAL DISTRIBUTION LIST

Combined Arms Research Library
US Army Command and General Staff College
250 Gibbon Ave.
Fort Leavenworth, KS 66027-2314

Defense Technical Information Center/OCA
825 John J. Kingman Rd., Suite 944
Fort Belvoir, VA 22060-6218

Harold S. Orenstein
Combined Arms Doctrine Directorate
USACGSC
1 Reynolds Ave.
Fort Leavenworth, KS 66027-1352

Lisa L. Cranford
Department of Logistics and Resource Operations
USACGSC
1 Reynolds Ave.
Fort Leavenworth, KS 66027-1352

Scott R. Peters
Combined Arms Doctrine Directorate
USACGSC
1 Reynolds Ave.
Fort Leavenworth, KS 66027-1352

Center for Strategic Leadership
US Army War College
650 Wright Avenue
Carlisle, PA 17013-5049

Ambassador Jim Dobbins
Dr. Bruce Hoffman
Dr. Bill Rosenau
1100 S. Hayes Street
Arlington, VA 22202

Dr. Peter Chalk
Dr. Ron Fricker
RAND
1700 Main Street, P.O. Box 2138
Santa Monica, CA 90404

CERTIFICATION FOR MMAS DISTRIBUTION STATEMENT

1. Certification Date: 18 June 2004

2. Thesis Author: MAJ Grady S. Taylor

3. Thesis Title: The Efficacy of the Instruments of National Power in Winning Insurgent Warfare: A Case Study Focused on Peru and Sendero Luminoso

4. Thesis Committee Members:
Signatures: _____
_____
_____

5. Distribution Statement: See distribution statements A-X on reverse, then circle appropriate distribution statement letter code below:

(A) B C D E F X   SEE EXPLANATION OF CODES ON REVERSE

If your thesis does not fit into any of the above categories or is classified, you must coordinate with the classified section at CARL.

6. Justification: Justification is required for any distribution other than described in Distribution Statement A. All or part of a thesis may justify distribution limitation. See limitation justification statements 1-10 on reverse, then list, below, the statement(s) that applies (apply) to your thesis and corresponding chapters/sections and pages. Follow sample format shown below:

EXAMPLE

Limitation Justification Statement	/	Chapter/Section	/	Page(s)
Direct Military Support (10)	/	Chapter 3	/	12
Critical Technology (3)	/	Section 4	/	31
Administrative Operational Use (7)	/	Chapter 2	/	13-32

Fill in limitation justification for your thesis below:

Limitation Justification Statement   /   Chapter/Section   /   Page(s)

_____ / _____ / _____
_____ / _____ / _____
_____ / _____ / _____
_____ / _____ / _____

7. MMAS Thesis Author's Signature: _____

STATEMENT A: Approved for public release; distribution is unlimited. (Documents with this statement may be made available or sold to the general public and foreign nationals).

STATEMENT B: Distribution authorized to US Government agencies only (insert reason and date ON REVERSE OF THIS FORM). Currently used reasons for imposing this statement include the following:

    1. Foreign Government Information. Protection of foreign information.

    2. Proprietary Information. Protection of proprietary information not owned by the US Government.

    3. Critical Technology. Protection and control of critical technology including technical data with potential military application.

    4. Test and Evaluation. Protection of test and evaluation of commercial production or military hardware.

    5. Contractor Performance Evaluation. Protection of information involving contractor performance evaluation.

    6. Premature Dissemination. Protection of information involving systems or hardware from premature dissemination.

    7. Administrative/Operational Use. Protection of information restricted to official use or for administrative or operational purposes.

    8. Software Documentation. Protection of software documentation - release only in accordance with the provisions of DoD Instruction 7930.2.

    9. Specific Authority. Protection of information required by a specific authority.

    10. Direct Military Support. To protect export-controlled technical data of such military significance that release for purposes other than direct support of DoD-approved activities may jeopardize a US military advantage.

STATEMENT C: Distribution authorized to US Government agencies and their contractors: (REASON AND DATE). Currently most used reasons are 1, 3, 7, 8, and 9 above.

STATEMENT D: Distribution authorized to DoD and US DoD contractors only; (REASON AND DATE). Currently most reasons are 1, 3, 7, 8, and 9 above.

STATEMENT E: Distribution authorized to DoD only; (REASON AND DATE). Currently most used reasons are 1, 2, 3, 4, 5, 6, 7, 8, 9, and 10.

STATEMENT F: Further dissemination only as directed by (controlling DoD office and date), or higher DoD authority. Used when the DoD originator determines that information is subject to special dissemination limitation specified by paragraph 4-505, DoD 5200.1-R.

STATEMENT X: Distribution authorized to US Government agencies and private individuals of enterprises eligible to obtain export-controlled technical data in accordance with DoD Directive 5230.25; (date). Controlling DoD office is (insert).

Milton Keynes UK
Ingram Content Group UK Ltd.
UKHW051821231023
431175UK00009B/741